MY
NEIGHBOR

MY
SISTER

MY
FRIEND

MY NEIGHBOR

MY SISTER

MY FRIEND

Ardeth Greene Kapp

BOOKCRAFT

Salt Lake City, Utah

BOOKCRAFT is a registered trademark of Deseret Book Company.

Visit us at deseretbook.com

First printed in hardbound 1990
First printed in paperbound 1995

Library of Congress Cataloging-in-Publication Data

Kapp, Ardeth Greene, 1931–
   My neighbor, my sister, my friend / by Ardeth Greene Kapp.
      p. cm
   ISBN 0-87579-299-5 (hardbound)
   ISBN 0-87579-958-2 (paperbound)
   1. Women—Religious life. 2. Women—Conduct of life. 3. Kapp,
Ardeth Greene, 1931–. I. Title
BV4527.K36 1990
248.8'43—dc20   89-71486
                                                   CIP

Printed in the United States of America   18961
R. R. Donnelley and Sons, Allentown, PA

20 19 18 17 16 15 14 13 12 11

*To all women — my neighbors,
my sisters, my friends: those whom I have
met and those whom I will yet meet as our
paths cross and our hearts reach out in love
and sisterhood while journeying toward
our heavenly home.*

Contents

Part IV

We Learn as We Live

Preface

We are all travelers for a time on this planet earth. One day we shall return to that dwelling place we knew before, and there rejoice in the memories of our journey and the experiences of this earth life—experiences some of which have taken us to the very mountain peaks of our lives and others into deep valleys as we have been tried and tested along the way, all for the purpose that we might be prepared to receive the glory the Lord has for us when we return. Sometimes we must trudge along in faith not knowing the answers for a time, but always knowing there is a divine plan and a purpose, and feeling the assurance of a loving Father in heaven. With this knowledge, we realize that the tests we are called upon to endure are for our growth, not to consume us but to refine us, not to discourage us but to enlighten us, and not to defeat us but to redeem us.

Some years ago I had a wonderful opportunity to travel to the Holy Land, the birthplace of our Lord and Savior, Jesus Christ. I walked where He had walked, and along the way I talked with friends, fellow travelers, of the things He taught. We shared feelings and emotions, testimonies, and tears of joy and gladness and some sadness. We drew strength from one another as we shared this memorable experience. Upon our return home, things were never quite the same again. Oh, the environment was the same and circumstances and challenges had not changed that much; but our thinking, our understanding, our vision had been expanded. We had been there together at the empty tomb, where we sang of the risen Christ and tried to comprehend what that singular experience meant to each of us in our own lives. We felt the mighty change of heart of which King Benjamin spoke and had a burning desire to "do good continually." (Mosiah 5:2.) The change that takes place is not in our circumstances but in the inner soul, when spirit speaks to spirit and the reality of our eternal relationship is very real. Through this unforgettable trip, a great bonding of friendship among the entire group has taken place, although we seldom see one another. But when we do meet, either as a group or individually, we try to relive all that we experienced. We exchange not just words but feelings. And while some of the memories grow dim, the feelings that we felt then seem to intensify, and we remember. We remember what we saw, but mostly we remember how we felt about the love and sacrifice of our Savior, about each other, about the very purpose of this earth life, and about our common commitment to follow the Savior. It was our love for Him that we had shared, and that feeling, once experienced, is never forgotten.

Since that time, there have been many, many trips with other travelers, not to Nazareth or Bethlehem, but through other cities and towns, with neighbors and sisters and friends journeying toward home, our heavenly home. We have met in conferences and firesides, large meetings and small. We have met in times of laughter and times of sadness, and witnessed an outpouring of the Spirit as our hearts have been touched by the glorious truths of the gospel of Jesus Christ. As we travel together through life, we learn to value differences of one another and treasure the uniqueness of each, knowing that we are all children of our Father in heaven. In the true spirit of sisterhood, we learn to reach out to one another and bear testimony of our common goals to return home—that home where we will not only walk where Jesus walks but will walk with Him and talk with Him. We will recall the times we traveled together, and we will remember.

Our common tie to this life may be a result of our date of birth and our allotted time on earth, or it may be geography, the place in which we live, that has brought us together for a time. But for all of us, wherever we live or whatever our circumstances may be, we share a common bond as sisters, members of the same family, through the gospel of Jesus Christ. It is with this feeling of being bonded together that I desire to draw closer to you, my neighbor, my sister, my friend, in full anticipation that when we return "home," we will have many occasions to remember when we traveled together, how we felt, and how we covenanted to help carry one another's burdens along the way. As we learn from the Doctrine and Covenants, "That same sociality which exists among us here will exist among us there, only it will be coupled with eternal glory, which glory we do not now enjoy." (D&C 130:2.) At that time, I believe, we will look back and, remembering our travels, will realize that what we identified as burdens along the way were not burdens at all, but lessons that qualified us to receive all the blessings our Father has promised us when we follow the path that leads us back to Him.

Recently I received a letter from a young woman who had attended a Young Women's conference attended by several hundred mothers and daughters. She wrote, "I waited in line after the meeting and you gave me a hug and said some wonderful things to me. I was the girl in the green jumper on the second row. Could you please write and tell me what you said. I forgot and I want to write it in my journal so I can read it when I'm feeling down." She didn't remember what was said, but she knew how she felt. It was a special moment when a relationship was established because of the spirit that was present, and she wanted to remember.

The joy of the journey comes through our relationships,

feelings for each other that, like divine echoes of times past, stir within us a quiet anticipation of the continuation of this same sociality eternally. It is as Alma told the people at the waters of Mormon: "Ye are desirous to come into the fold of God, and to be called his people, and are willing to bear one another's burdens, that they may be light; yea, and are willing to mourn with those that mourn; yea, and comfort those that stand in need of comfort, and to stand as witnesses of God at all times and in all things, and in all places that ye may be in, even until death, that ye may be redeemed of God, and be numbered with those of the first resurrection, that ye may have eternal life." (Mosiah 18:8–9.)

Over the years, I have received many letters from my sisters, young and old, not unlike the request from the little girl "in the green jumper on the second row." It is in response to these kinds of expressions that I desire to share the messages in these chapters and would, if I could, give you a hug and "say some wonderful things" to you—my neighbor, my sister, my friend.

Acknowledgments

I express appreciation to my husband, Heber, who believes I can write, encourages me to write, and makes time for me to write. I am grateful to Kerry Lin Hammond, a very able and efficient secretary, who typed many drafts along the way toward the completion of this project. And I express deepest gratitude and appreciation to Eleanor Knowles, executive editor of Deseret Book, who first encouraged me to publish and who has provided the skillful editing for this manuscript.

Part I

Away from Our Heavenly Home

Chapter 1

That We May Prepare to Do Our Part

Some time ago when I was shopping for groceries, as we all do, a woman saw me and asked, in a tone of surprise, "Do you buy groceries?" I smiled and said, "Yes, and I eat them too."

We are all so ordinary, and yet each is special and unique. It is when we come to know that we are literally sisters in the same family away from our heavenly home for a time that we begin to really recognize each other—not in relation to positions, possessions, prestige, or power, but rather as sisters, heart to heart and soul to soul. Then when we meet we don't exchange just words, but a wonderful exchange of the spirit takes place. We learn to share and trust and risk and not be so concerned about what we do but rather who we are and, even more important, *whose* we are. We begin to reveal how we feel. We laugh together and cry together and learn how to bear one another's burdens so that they may be light. At least that is what we, as covenant people, hope to do—and yet at times we fall short of the mark and feel some disappointment in ourselves because we are not always doing as well as we could or should or would, given another chance. But above all, it is important for you to know you and me to know me.

On occasion when we conduct a private and sometimes sobering interview with ourselves, we recognize the distance between the ideal and the real. It humbles us and increases our desire for an improved performance, given the wonderful gift of another day. We all hope for the final commendation on our performance, "Well done, thou good and faithful servant."

When the Promised Valley Playhouse in Salt Lake City announced a few years ago that it was going to produce the musical play *Annie*, 320 young girls auditioned for the part of Annie. Not everyone who tried out got a part, and some who got parts didn't get the ones they thought they wanted. Following a period of intensive rehearsals, the opening night was absolutely spectacular, and the girl who played the lead took many well-deserved bows. But as magnificent as Annie's performance was, her greatest moment, I believe, came after the show, when she graciously acknowledged praises from throngs of admirers in the lobby of the theater. In a corner of the lobby I observed an elderly gentleman, stooped with age and his eyes moist, eagerly searching the crowd. Somehow, through a small opening in the crowd, Annie caught a glimpse of the old man. Forgetting all the public acclaim and with arms outstretched she called, "Grandpa, Grandpa!" The crowd parted, leaving a narrow passageway for this precious moment. The elderly man reached out his arms like parentheses and nestled his precious granddaughter close to him. He spoke softly, and although I could not hear, I think he must have said, "My dear, you played your part so very, very well."

Since that memorable occasion, I have replayed that scene in my mind many times and contemplated the greeting we will each receive following our final performance. Each of us is on stage for a time. This is not the first nor the final act. It is the second act, and we have been assured that we performed our first act very well. Concerning the second, our Father in heaven has said, "We will prove them herewith, to see if they will do all things whatsoever the Lord their God shall command them; and they who keep their first estate shall be added upon; . . . and they who keep their second estate shall have glory added upon their heads for ever and ever." (Abraham 3:25–26.)

As we participate in this great drama of earth life, we often find that the parts we so much desire may not be available to us for a time. We find ourselves placed in other roles, only to discover after some years and after a trial of our faith that those other roles may even be the very ones we auditioned for, roles for which we received coaching and divine guidance from our Heavenly Father before we left our heavenly home to come on stage for a season.

President George Q. Cannon gives us great insight as he explains, "God has chosen us out of the world and has given us a great mission. I do not entertain a doubt myself that we were selected and fore-ordained for the mission before the world was, that we had our parts allotted to us in this mortal state of existence as our Savior had His assigned to Him." (*Gospel Truth* [Deseret Book, 1987], p. 18.)

In the production of *Annie,* Sandy, Annie's dog, broke loose, missed his cue, and entered too soon. He could have spoiled the show, but Annie came to the rescue and helped him wait until it was his time to enter. As participants on the stage of life, we too must be sensitive to timing, and we must work to support each other. There are times when some will, for a brief moment, move center stage in front of the lights, then go backstage or even offstage into the wings for a time, confident that the entire cast will participate in the final curtain call.

I believe that the sensitivity we each have for another's part, major or minor, will affect tremendously the quality of our individual and final performance. And it is often in the supportive roles that we see the finest and most magnificent examples.

This analogy of being onstage with a particular part is

not intended to suggest that anyone performs as a puppet on a string. This would violate the basic doctrine of agency, which is so critical to the very purpose of earth life. And yet many young people whom I talk to, and sometimes older ones, mistakenly believe that they should wait for a prompting of the Spirit on every decision. They believe that if things go well, it is because the Spirit prompts them on what to do, and if things don't go well, it is because the devil made them do it.

President Brigham Young gives us some great insight into our responsibility for choosing well. He said, "God is the author of all good; and yet, if you rightly understood yourselves, you would not directly attribute every good act you perform to our Father in heaven, nor to his Son Jesus Christ, nor to the Holy Ghost; neither would you attribute every evil act of a man or woman to the Devil or his spirits or influences; for man is organized by his Creator to act perfectly independently of all influences there are above or beneath. Those influences are always attending him, and are ready to dictate and direct—to lead him into truth or to lead him to destruction. But is he always guided by those influences in every act? He is not. It is ordained of God that we should act independently in and of ourselves, and the good is present when we need it. If we will ask for it, it is with us." (*Journal of Discourses* 9:122.)

We are responsible for our own actions. We are always at liberty to ad lib and be distracted by seemingly more exciting things. For example, some of us may spend so much time in the wardrobe department selecting, designing, modeling, combining this with that, including all the accessories, that we may miss our cue. Others may be distracted by the props, the scenery, the set. But these, although important in their place, pale by comparison to the joy that comes in touching another's life in some quiet, small act of service. Would we ever let our possessions stand in the way of that joy which comes when we share our lives with others?

Even as we endeavor to play our various parts in their appropriate seasons, there will continually be self-appointed stage managers who, not knowing or caring about the script, will shout from the wings, "You're playing the wrong part. You don't want the supporting role. That isn't important. Why be a supporting actor when you can be the star? Be front stage. Move in. Let them know who you are. This is your chance to win the applause."

There are those who would attempt to revise, rewrite, and restructure the script, changing the sacred roles of men and women, modifying the scenes and seasons, adjusting the morals and models where possible, and even altering the main stage, the home, in which the most important drama of life should unfold.

There are always loud voices assuming authorship while abdicating stewardship. You and I may never win acclaim, and society may never know us beyond the street where we live, or because one calling or position may be in the public eye more than another. But I am sure that when the lights have gone out and the curtain is closed on our second act, the opinions of others, the acceptance and applause of the crowd, will be a haunting echo if our Father's approval is in question.

It won't matter if we play center stage or in the wings if our Lord and Savior is at the very center of our life. He reaches out to us with this promise: "Look unto me in every thought; doubt not, fear not. Behold the wounds which pierced my side, and also the prints of the nails in my hands and feet; be faithful, keep my commandments and ye shall inherit the kingdom of heaven." (D&C 6:36–37.) And Alma reminds us, "This life is the time for men to prepare to meet God; yea, behold the day of this life is the day for men to perform their labors." (Alma 34:32.) Our labors come in a variety of ways.

Recently I visited with a young woman in her early twenties. She poured out her heart, saying, "If I were just pretty, then I'd feel more confident." It is so easy to be distracted by vanity and pride. I believe that is one of the reasons that we have more than three hundred references in the scriptures to the word *remember.* When we remember our parts, when we remember who we are and whose we are, we are no longer distracted by foolish intruders. Remember Alma's question to those who would gain exaltation: "I ask of you, my brethren [I might add sisters] of the church, have ye spiritually been born of God? Have ye received his image in your countenances? Have ye experienced this mighty change in your hearts?" (Alma 5:14.) When this takes place, our beauty will be unsurpassed and assured.

Of course, it is appropriate that we look our best, but before we become dazzled with the glamour of our outer wear, we might heed the words of Alma: "Yea, can ye be puffed up in the pride of your hearts; yea, will ye still persist in the wearing of costly apparel and setting your hearts upon the vain things of the world, upon your riches?" (Alma 5:53.) There are many attractive distractions that would interfere, if they could, with our command performance.

When we let go of our sins and our eye is single to the glory of God, we are promised that our whole body shall be filled with light and that there shall be no darkness in us. (D&C 88:67.) We will hear the still, small voice prompting us from the wings, reminding us of our lines day by day. And even when we may question our own strength and ability, we can take comfort in the promises of the Lord when we are on His errand: "I will go before your face. I will be on your right hand and on your left, and my Spirit shall be in your hearts, and mine angels round about you, to bear you up." (D&C 84:88.)

Some years ago my husband, Heber, and I arose early to go to the laying of the cornerstone for the Jordan River Temple. We planned to arrive well before the crowd, but our plan was ill timed. The crowd was already there when we arrived. Due to the contour of the land, I was not only stretching to see over the heads of those in front of me, but we were on the low side of the slope in front of the temple, and I couldn't see what was going on. Heber, being considerably taller, tried to ease my disappointment by reporting to me observations from his vantage point. "The choir is assembling," he reported. "The General Authorities are taking their places. The TV cameras are in place." This only added to my frustration as I faced the backs of those in front who were seeing this historic event that I was missing.

After reaching and stretching without success, I decided to settle down, hoping to just feel the spirit of the occasion. It was when I relaxed that my perspective changed and I noticed an activity at the far northeast side of the temple. There I observed two men dressed in dark pants, white shirts, and ties, and each was holding a shovel. I saw them empty sacks of concrete into a wheelbarrow, pour in water, and mix the contents.

In time, after the choir sang and the presiding authorities had delivered impressive messages, Heber reported that the cameras were moving to the location for the placement of the cornerstone. At that moment the men who had been mixing the mortar pushed the wheelbarrow forward and quickly disappeared behind the scene. Then the cornerstone was anchored in place.

On the television news that evening, I saw what the cameras saw. But they did not see what I had seen. And even today, years later, I never drive past the Jordan River Temple without thinking of those men who mixed the mortar—those whose quiet, unsung labors played a major role in the placement of the cornerstone for the House of the Lord in a building that will stand against all the storms of life.

Given a choice, would you be willing to serve with the men who mix the mortar? Small acts of service, small sacrifices, small notes and calls, words of encouragement one to another—these "small things" are the mortar that help hold life together.

The routine of life may sometimes seem a little humdrum, repetitious, and routine, maybe even boring on occasion. We must not let that happen. It is all right to get tired, but we should never become bored with life. How long has it been since you have celebrated the dawn of a new day, studied the dew on a spider web, or counted the petals on a daisy? Oh, that we may remain alive and alert as long as we live!

At times when my role seems difficult and when there are more demands than I can meet, I am forced to set priorities because I can't do it all. Then I read again the words of our Savior, words that help me as I try to separate the urgent demands from the vital virtues: "A new commandment I give unto you, That ye love one another; as I have loved you, that ye also love one another. By this shall all men know that ye are my disciples, if ye have love one to another." (John 13:34–35.)

Our greatest performances come when we take time to give of ourselves in love, one for another, often away from the crowd. Of the multitude of happenings during the past several years in my life, may I share what I would like to have recorded on a page of history as possibly a noteworthy performance.

A few years ago, as Christmas drew near, I found myself confronted with a very full schedule. The streets were crowded, my calendar was crowded, and my mind was crowded. There was so much to do and so little time. An invitation to give a brief Christmas message to the residents of a nursing home nearby was one activity I could check off rather quickly and then move to the next appointment.

As I rushed past the receptionist at the nursing home door, I was ushered into a large room where I suddenly stopped. Life was moving at a different pace here, if it was moving at all. There were wheelchairs, bent shoulders, gray hair, tired eyes, and the impression of so little going on. Though the room was warm, many of the elderly had knitted shawls draped over rounded shoulders and woolly slippers covering tired feet.

Following my message, one of the visitors, the granddaughter of one of the elderly residents, asked if I had time to visit with her grandmother in her own private room for just a few moments. She commented, "She thinks she knows you," indicating perhaps that her grandmother's mind might also be tired. I agreed that I could spare a few minutes, and I followed the younger woman as she helped her elderly grandmother shuffle down the narrow hall to her room. When she reached her bedside, this dear elderly woman slowly turned around, let go of her granddaughter's arm, and sat on her bed. Then she raised her head so that I could look into her face. My eyes caught hers. "Sister Myrtle Dudley!" I exclaimed. "You were my Primary teacher."

Her wrinkled mouth formed a smile as she pulled on her granddaughter's jacket and said, "See, I told you she would know me."

I continued, "I remember when you used to lead the singing. You wore that wine-colored dress with the big sleeves that waved back and forth as you taught us the songs."

Again she pulled on her granddaughter's jacket. "I told you she would know me."

"Yes," I said, "and you made carrot juice for my mother when she was sick."

Then she asked, "Did you come all the way from Canada just to see me?"

"Oh, Sister Dudley," I said, "I have come a long way. It has been over forty years."

She reached out her arms and drew me close. I felt like a child once again, back in Primary, in the arms of my teacher who loved me. Then she whispered in my ear, "I knew you would know me."

There in the arms of my Primary teacher the world stood still for a moment. The busy streets were forgotten. The crowded calendar was no longer pressing on my mind. The spirit of Christmas filled my soul. A small miracle was taking place, not because of what I brought but because of what I received.

After a time, I reluctantly left the presence of my Primary teacher and walked slowly back to my car. I sat there pondering while the snowflakes fell gently on the windshield. It was the season of celebration for the birth of Jesus Christ, our Lord and Savior. It was He who asked us to love one another and to serve one another. He said to each of us, "Inasmuch as ye have done it unto one of the least of these my brethren, ye have done it unto me." (Matthew 25:40.)

Yes, I thought, I knew Sister Dudley because she had served me, and she knew me because she had served me. Then the vision cleared before my eyes. We will know Him when we serve Him, and He will know us when we serve Him. And I asked myself, Can I one day say with the same confidence with which Sister Dudley spoke, "I told you He would know me"?

Let us always keep in mind an anticipation of that glorious day when we will be with our Father again. The words of President George Q. Cannon help us envision that event: "We existed with Him in a family relationship as His children. . . . When we see our Father in heaven we shall know Him; and the recollection that we were once with Him and that He was our Father will come back to us, and we will fall upon His neck, and He will fall upon us, and we will kiss each other. We will know our Mother, also." (*Gospel Truth,* pp. 1, 3.)

One day, like Annie, we will leave the stage. I am confident that, having done our part, we will receive an embrace and experience the greatest commendation we could ever hope for from the only one who really matters. "You played your part so very, very well," I believe we will hear our

Father and Mother say, "My child, I have you home again."
Then we will hear not with our ears, but with our spirit, the
echoing applause of multitudes of heavenly hosts, our
brothers and our sisters, rejoicing in our safe return to have
glory added upon our heads forever and ever.

May we find our constant example in that part played
by the greatest model in the greatest moment of all time.
May the curtain never close until our work is finished. And
when it does close, may we each feel the satisfaction of having listened to the whisperings of the Spirit every day of our
lives, that we may prepare to do our part.

Chapter 2

The Promise of Tomorrow

An old farmer, asked how he was, reportedly said, "I am better than I was but I ain't as good as I'm going to be." I believe that tomorrow's promise rests in that philosophy. We are better than we were but not as good as we are going to be, and that suggests growth and progress and even some discomfort and struggle.

Have you ever seen a tree cut down or looked at the end of a log that has been cut? On the trunk, a pattern of growth rings represents each year of the tree's life. Our own lives may be similar to that of the tree. Some of our seasons provide wider growth rings than others. Some are not as wide. During some of our days, we may not do as much and may just want to slow down or wait.

Let me share with you three approaches to handling growth and change and our tomorrows. To illustrate the first, do you remember the famous book *Gone with the Wind?* Scarlett O'Hara, in times of great stress, uses a phrase that is characteristic of her approach to facing difficult challenges. "I won't think about that now," she says. "I'll think of it all tomorrow. . . . After all, tomorrow is another day."

We see another approach in the popular play *Annie.* Annie, an orphan child, is mistreated, abandoned, and neglected, with no real evidence of having a brighter future. But in Annie's mind she has hope; she has faith. As she sings those famous words, "The sun will come out tomorrow," she lifts and leads herself and others out of the darkness of their despair into the sunshine of hope. Annie doesn't know what tomorrow will bring, but there is no question of her unwavering optimism.

The third approach is found in the musical *The Unsinkable Molly Brown*. We see Molly at the beginning as a backwoods girl with few opportunities, no education, and no refinement. While wrestling with her adopted brothers she is pinned down, and one of them yells, "You're down, Molly! You're down!" Molly responds, "I ain't down! And even if I was, you'd sure never hear it from me 'cause I hate the word *down*, but I love the word *up* 'cause that means hope. And that's what I got. Hope for someplace prettier and someplace cleaner. And if I gotta eat catfish heads all my life, can't I eat them off a plate and in a red silk dress?"

Scarlett O'Hara tells us something about waiting for another day if we cannot handle any more today, and that is an important lesson. We can live with the hope and maybe a promise that tomorrow will be better, since it may seem at times that it can't possibly get any worse. Annie has great faith, knowing that as bad as things are, the sun *will* shine tomorrow. And that's only a day away. But Molly Brown won't wait until tomorrow. She believes that the promise of tomorrow rests in her hands today. She refuses to be down for even a day—and even if she were down, no one would know it. Molly realizes that if happiness is dependent on tomorrow, then when tomorrow comes she can still be living in expectation of a better day. She plans for tomorrow by taking care of today.

Each of us needs to determine to do all we can to fill our days with hope and faith and happiness now. In the Book of Mormon we read, "And then cometh the time that . . . he that is righteous shall be righteous still; he that is happy shall be happy still; and he that is unhappy shall be unhappy still." (Mormon 9:14.)

Does that suggest that the promise of a happy future is

in question if things aren't going well for us today? I think not. My own experience teaches me that the promise of happiness today and tomorrow is not necessarily an escape from turmoil, anguish, or disappointment or from trials or tests of any kind. In fact, quite the contrary. If we qualify for all that is promised tomorrow, we *must* be tried and tested today.

The Lord has told us, "My people must be tried in all things, that they may be prepared to receive the glory that I have for them, even the glory of Zion; and he that will not bear chastisement is not worthy of my kingdom." (D&C 136:31.)

President Marion G. Romney once said, "I am convinced that if we are to have peace in our hearts, we must learn how to preserve it in our hearts in the midst of trouble and trial." How can we do this when the harsh winters of our lives seem for a season to give little hope of spring? How can we hold on when the voices of the world shout alluring promises about tomorrow and offer escape and freedom from the responsibilities of today?

It is not the loud voices of the world, or even the murmuring of troubled men and women, that we must tune our ears to, but the quiet whisperings of the Spirit. When we are clear in our minds and in our hearts concerning the promises made by the Lord to each of us, we can fill our minds with gospel truths and close out those conflicting thoughts that can erode our faith and destroy our peace.

In Proverbs we read, "For as [a man] thinketh in his heart, so is he." (Proverbs 23:7.) We find ourselves today where yesterday's thoughts have brought us. We cannot escape the harvest of the seeds we plant. Tomorrow's promise, then, rests with our thoughts today. In contrast, those who expose their minds to things that are disquieting to the Spirit can expect to be unsettled, unsure, unsatisfied, and unhappy tomorrow.

In the *Deseret News* recently I read about Deborah

McKeithan, who is legally blind and an epileptic and has partial paralysis and cerebral multiple sclerosis. " 'In fact,' she chuckles, 'the only thing that works really well is my mouth.' Colleagues add to the list 'her heart, her head and her highly developed stubborn streak and determination.'" Despite her problems, however, Deborah says, "I'm a disabled person working very hard not to let my attitude be my handicap."

Here are a few thoughts that could be used to cultivate a feeling of misery today and tomorrow, if we were to choose to think that way:

1. Fill your mind with thoughts of the things you don't have and wish you had while ignoring all that you do have.

2. Think about and talk about yourself.

3. Ponder your own weaknesses as you compare yourself with the obvious strengths of those around you.

4. Think one way and act another.

5. Insist on consideration and respect from others.

6. Blame others for making you feel unhappy.

7. Sulk if people are not grateful to you for all you have done.

8. Never forget a service you may have rendered.

9. Be full of pride.

10. Be sensitive to slights.

11. Be jealous and envious.

12. Never forget a criticism.

13. Trust nobody but yourself. Be ungrateful.

14. Request that the epitaph on your tombstone read "I told you I was sick."

Why do some of these thoughts attack our minds like a relentless enemy? How do we fight against them? The mind is always working; it never stops. Let us guard against the subtle inroads today that can become embedded habits of negativism tomorrow. We will find our strength and our peace when we study and pray and ponder and meditate, and when we strive to listen to the whisperings of the Spirit. This course will provide undeviating, constant answers to our most basic questions concerning our identity. "Who am I?"; our direction, "What am I to do?"; and our reason for being, "What is the purpose of my life?"

To follow such a course, we need some time each day when we can be alone and can tell the Lord just how things are with us. We need a time to review our promises and covenants in private with Him, a time when we, in a way, hold an interview concerning our lives up to this point. We each need this time to ponder our blessings and the words of the Lord in the scriptures and thereby increase our understanding. On occasion, we will experience an unfolding and an awakening, as it were, of things we have known before, a "divine echo." We need these very personal, quiet, sacred moments. It is a time of pulling ourselves together and away from the influences that pull us apart. What matters is that we become inwardly attentive, so that when the outside noise of life is quieted, there is an inner music of our very own. Then when people knock on the door of our soul, they will find someone is at home.

In our quiet times, we can count our blessings and come to know who we are and, more importantly, whose we are. Not infrequently people will come up to me, thinking they recognize me, and say, "You're Sister Kapp, aren't you?" And I will reply, "Yes, I am." Then in sincere interest I'll ask, "And who are you?" Too often the answer is, "Oh, I'm nobody." And right then I feel an intense desire to mount a platform and, with the fervor of an evangelist, plead for them to have the vision of who they really are—that their eyes might be open and they might see with their heart and soul.

How I wish that all people, young and old, could see themselves as they really are. Each one is a wonderful human being, the offspring of Deity, a son or daughter of God. When I hear comments of self-depreciation, I want to open my scriptures and read to them from the fifth chapter of Mosiah:

"And now, because of the covenant which ye have made ye shall be called the children of Christ, his sons, and his daughters; for behold, this day he hath spiritually begotten you; for ye say that your hearts are changed through faith on his name; therefore, ye are born of him and have become his sons and his daughters.

"And under this head ye are made free, and there is no other head whereby ye can be made free. There is no other name given whereby salvation cometh; therefore, I would that ye should take upon you the name of Christ, all you that have entered into the covenant with God that ye should be obedient unto the end of your lives. . . .

"Therefore, I would that ye should be steadfast and immovable, always abounding in good works, that Christ, the Lord God Omnipotent, may seal you his, that you may be brought to heaven, that ye may have everlasting salvation and eternal life, through the wisdom, and power, and justice, and mercy of him who created all things, in heaven and in earth, who is God above all." (Mosiah 5:7–8, 15.)

A knowledge of these eternal truths can quiet our restless nature when we feel less than we are. This knowledge makes the steep and steady climb upward one of adventure and hope, not despair.

It doesn't matter who we aren't when we know who we are. We are the children of God. He is our Father. Think of it! The promise of tomorrow rests with our knowing who our Eternal Father is and knowing that there is no attribute we ascribe to Him that we do not possess, though it may be dormant or in embryo. Knowing this eternal truth brings a warm and exciting, yet weighty and humbling, sense of responsibility that forces the question, Then what am I to do?

One thing we are commanded to do is to "seek learning, even by study and also by faith." (D&C 88:118.) We are taught that "whatever principle of intelligence we attain unto in this life, it will rise with us in the resurrection. And if a person gains more knowledge and intelligence in this life through his diligence and obedience than another, he will have so much the advantage in the world to come." (D&C 130:18–19.) We are here to succeed. If we pray for help and study diligently, we will find that our minds will be enlightened and receptive to things that we could not grasp previously.

Sometimes questions are raised about the value of education for women. I believe education presupposes the wise use of knowledge and that the wise use of knowledge will help us reach our eternal goals.

When we each have the promises of eternity indelibly imprinted in our mind, our heart, and our soul, and our understanding of the purpose of life is firmly in place, then our plans, our education, and our preparation for tomorrow can move ahead safely, because we will measure every decision in relation to our eternal values and our ultimate destination. When these values are in place, we can manage our education wisely and without threat to our highest and ultimate goals. Personal revelation is involved in this process. Timing is critical, and an ear tuned to the words of the living prophet provides guidance and safety.

We are not able to do all things at once, but, guided by the Spirit, we can set our priorities and refuse to let enticing opportunities rob us of our ultimate goals. We need to avoid detours and delays that may appear to be appealing, enticing, and rewarding. We must learn to resist rationalization and hold fast to those things which are most dear.

Sometimes in the spirit of intellectual excitement, with our knowledge, experience, and wisdom increasing, we may find ourselves feeling the need to evaluate, assess, and analyze every principle, every truth, and every guideline ever given, even by the Prophet himself. Many years ago, I sat listening to several of my intellectual friends discussing issues that raised questions in my mind about some of the things I had always accepted. I remember feeling that if I were to be as smart as they, maybe I should be wondering and asking more of those kinds of questions—questions that addressed the very fundamentals of my belief. Then one day I realized that that was not only unnecessary, it was unwise. If I was going to progress, I must be true to what I had already come to know was right. Then I would expand my knowledge and search for answers to more things and build on the sure foundation I had already put in place. Tomorrow is not built by casting stones at the foundation of what we have put in place today. We don't need to keep pulling up a plant to see if its roots are still there.

There seems to be a tendency for some to be forever testing even the basic truths to see if they are real or worthwhile. Some truths, feelings, and thoughts have to be accepted on face value, at least for the moment. We don't need to be completely gullible, but a constant pecking away at even the strongest foundation can eventually destroy it. Sometimes a person's desire to question everyone and everything is not so much a measure of that person's lack of confidence in others but the lack of security within himself.

Everywhere we hear many voices, and many opinions and weighty decisions must be made along the way. When we remember who our Father is, who we are, and that tomorrow's promise will return us to our heavenly home, then the attractive detours for even a brief delay lose their glamour, their appeal, and their temptation. The Lord has told us, "I, the Lord, am bound when ye do what I say; but when ye do not what I say, ye have no promise." (D&C 82:10.) He gives us the commandments out of His infinite love for us, because the commandments of God are the laws through which we make ourselves receptive to the guidance and comfort and protection of the Holy Ghost. This is the gift given of our Father, to bring us safely home. We keep the commandments so that we can have His Spirit to be with us.

We read in the Doctrine and Covenants, "Verily, thus saith the Lord: It shall come to pass that every soul who forsaketh his sins and cometh unto me, and calleth on my name, and obeyeth my voice, and keepeth my commandments, shall see my face and know that I am." (D&C 93:1.) The Lord wants us to get the spirit and the vision and understand the purpose of our earthly mission.

One day we shall return home and our Father will say, "My child, I have you home again." And we will know our Father and His Son, Jesus Christ, our Elder Brother. Tomorrow's promise brings eternal life through our Savior's infinite and eternal atonement. He paid the price for us to come forth from the grave and gives us His glorious promise: "Because I live, ye shall live also." (John 14:19.) He has invited all to come unto Him. He will guide us safely home.

Chapter 3

Our Inheritance:
Secure or in Jeopardy?

Some months ago I attended a missionary farewell in another ward. After a few words of greeting, the opening song, and the invocation, the bishop attended to some ward business. Then, looking out across the congregation, he asked, "Chad, are you here?"

Immediately the sound of a folding chair knocked noisily against another could be heard, and a young boy made his way awkwardly into the aisle. As he turned to maneuver by, I observed from his facial features that he might not have the same mental abilities of other young people his age. I watched as he literally ran, awkwardly but with great enthusiasm, up the full length of the chapel. On the stand the bishop put his arm around Chad and drew him close for a moment, the two of them looking at each other with a private exchange only they understood. Then, with Chad nestled securely in the fold of his arm, the bishop announced to the audience, "Chad has earned his Duty to God award. He has qualified in every way." Glancing down at the young man, he added, with deep feeling, "We're all proud of you, Chad."

Following the presentation there was the usual handshake and an additional warm and sustained embrace. As Chad turned to leave, he broke with tradition and raised his hand high in the air. The bishop understood the signal and responded to Chad's invitation by raising his hand to meet Chad's, giving a resounding clap in the air. Outside the meeting he would probably have added the words, "Give me five."

Before leaving the stand, Chad walked quickly toward the chorister, who stood and wrapped him in his arms. I learned later that the man was his father. Then the young boy made his way down the aisle with a broad smile on his face and his arm raised high in the air as if to "give 'em five" to every ward member who had helped him and who now shared in his victory.

It has been months since that memorable Sunday, but in my mind I keep playing that scene over and over again. What struggles and challenges preceded that day for Chad? Were there times when he might have wanted to give up? Certainly some of the requirements must have been harder for him than they were for others his age. Were there times of discouragement and maybe disappointment? He was smiling when the bishop called him forward to receive his Duty to God award, but there must have been many times when even duty to God was difficult. I wonder if there were times when Chad, in the privacy of his own heart, asked the Father why—why does it have to be so hard? And while he waited for the answer, he kept going.

Each of us has circumstances that might seem like handicaps, not necessarily like Chad's, but challenges that test our courage and strength, our commitment and ultimately our faith in a loving Heavenly Father. And how do we respond?

A bishop calls. The call is heard and people respond. Those who have learned to listen for the call are prepared and ready to respond. They don't wait, they don't walk, they don't stop to explain, they don't ask why. However wearisome the test or whatever the circumstances, however severe the handicaps or steep the road, still many prepare to come running when they are called.

As we learn to listen and follow the counsel of the Lord, both written and spoken, we prepare for that day when there will be a call for each of us—a call to come home, not later when we are better prepared, but now. We might hear the words, "Come, my child. Come as you are, but come now." With unwavering faith in our ultimate reward and our divine inheritance as rightful heirs, will we, like Chad, be prepared to run forward with confidence when we hear that call?

In the Book of Mormon Alma invites us to envision the alternative: "Can you imagine to yourselves that ye hear the voice of the Lord, saying unto you, in that day: Come unto me ye blessed, for behold, your works have been the works of righteousness upon the face of the earth? . . . Or otherwise, can ye imagine yourselves brought before the tribunal of God with your souls filled with guilt and remorse, having a remembrance of all your guilt, yea, a perfect remembrance of all your wickedness, yea, a remembrance that ye have set at defiance the commandments of God? I say unto you, can ye look up to God at that day with a pure heart and clean hands? I say unto you, can ye look up, having the image of God engraven upon your countenances?" (Alma 5:18–19.)

The answers to these questions are found in the choices we make. Every choice counts one way or the other. We are free to choose to follow or not to follow, to abide the law or to disregard it, to have freedom or to forfeit it, to claim our inheritance or to leave it unclaimed.

Recently I was asked to speak to a gathering of men in a small chapel. These men had an understanding of law, agency, freedom, blessings, choice, and accountability. To reach the chapel I had to go through tight security, present identification, and be escorted by an officer of the law down a long corridor and through sets of metal doors that sounded a haunting echo as metal clanged against metal. Each door in sequence closed tightly behind me, and I knew I was locked in.

As I approached the chapel, I heard a sound that seemed foreign to that setting—beautiful male voices singing in harmony and with great feeling. I entered the meeting, which was already in session, and observed each man wearing a uniform that had an identification number across the left side of the chest. Most of them were holding hymnbooks, and they were singing the hymn "How Gentle God's Commands." I'll never hear that hymn again without reliving that experience. These are the words:

> *How gentle God's commands!*
> *How kind his precepts are!*
> *Come, cast your burdens on the Lord*
> *And trust his constant care.*
>
> *Beneath his watchful eye,*
> *His Saints securely dwell;*
> *That hand which bears all nature up*
> *Shall guard his children well.*
>
> *Why should this anxious load*
> *Press down your weary mind?*
> *Haste to your Heav'nly Father's throne*
> *And sweet refreshment find.*
>
> *His goodness stands approved,*
> *Unchanged from day to day;*
> *I'll drop my burden at his feet*
> *And bear a song away.*

As I shook hands with one of the inmates, I looked into his sad eyes and wondered: My brother, when did you begin to exercise your agency, your freedom, and, little by little, to move from freedom to enslavement and finally imprisonment? Did you not know that you were an heir with a birthright, a divine inheritance? Did you realize you were moving in this direction? Did it begin in high school when the influence of peers spoke louder than the wisdom of parents? Or was it the freedom from parents into the environment of college or work that opened a door that appeared to be freedom and has now closed and locked behind you? When did the chains that bind begin to form just one small link at a time? Who else shares in the responsibility? Is it perhaps that I am not only my brother's keeper but also my brother's maker? What is the effect of my influence on those around me?

As children of God, we are His heirs. But we must first be tested before we can be trusted with our inheritance— the power and blessings of God our Eternal Father. Then we can become joint-heirs with Jesus Christ, with glory added upon our heads forever and ever.

When we have a spiritual perspective and come to fully understand our promised blessings, our inheritance, and the mission of the Savior and the price He paid in our behalf to help us claim our reward, I believe that even on our hardest days our tests will hardly seem severe enough. It seems unfathomable that after the price paid by Him because of His great love for us, we are still free to choose whether or not that sacrifice in our behalf is accepted or rejected. We are given our agency.

As we are tried and tempered in the furnace of affliction, it is not to consume us but to refine us, to qualify us, to prove us. Our severe tests are designed to try us. The temptations and testing begin very early in life and continue so long as we dwell in this mortal state. It begins something like this:

My nephew, Kent, was pleading with his mom just before lunchtime to go over to his friend's to play. "No," his mother said, "not now."

Kent went outside to his sandpile to ponder. Something in the inherent nature of everyone reaches out for freedom and a desire to exercise agency. Suddenly he went running back into the house. "Mom," he asked, "what if I go to Dougie's anyway?"

"Then I guess I would have to discipline you for disobeying."

"What would you do?"

Pressed for an answer, and without much time to

ponder the magnitude of the disobedience, she said, "I guess I'd have to spank you."

He thought momentarily and then inquired further before making his decision. "Would it be with my pants up or on my bare bottom?"

His mom was not quite prepared for this response, but she said, "I guess it would be with your pants up."

"How many times?"

"Five," she said.

"Five!" he exclaimed. "Five for just going to Dougie's? That's not fair."

"It might not seem fair," she explained, "but that's how it is. You suit yourself."

He needed more information before he made a decision. "Can I go after lunch?" he asked.

"Kent, if you choose to be obedient and not go over to Dougie's, then after lunch we'll do something even better. You can go with me to pick up your daddy."

Kent had not known of that alternative. With that in the plan, the desire to go to his friend's was of little consequence. He used his agency, was spared the spanking, and participated in an even more desirable activity.

Sometimes we are shortsighted and are not aware of what awaits us just around the corner following our obedience. We "receive no witness until after the trial of [our] faith." (Ether 12:6.) But we don't negotiate with our Father in heaven on these matters. The laws are in place. We know that "there is a law . . . upon which all blessings are predicated," and when we receive any blessing, "it is by obedience to that law." (D&C 130:20.)

And so our Father, wanting us to qualify for all of the blessings, has given us laws and commandments. These commandments are given not to restrict us but to redeem us; not just to reform us but to exalt us. "Therefore," as Nephi said, "cheer up your hearts, and remember that ye are free to act for yourselves—to choose the way of everlasting death or the way of eternal life." (2 Nephi 10:23.)

Some of us resent, resist, even recoil from the apparent restrictions imposed upon us. And so it was in the Savior's time. There were those who didn't like what he taught. "This is an hard saying; who can hear it?" they said. "When Jesus knew in himself that his disciples murmured at it, he said unto them, Doth this offend you?" And we read that "from that time many of his disciples went back, and walked no more with him." (John 6:60–61, 66.)

There are, at least in the minds of some, too many rules, too many commandments, honor codes, all kinds of regulations, standards, and restrictions. These serve as constant reminders. And leaders who love us and believe in us will give of their time to meet with us at regular intervals and help remind us of what we have the capacity to become. Especially in times of discouragement, trials, and tests, they will help us, carry our burdens, and believe in us when we may otherwise not even believe in ourselves. Obedience is the key that unlocks the door and sets us free.

I am reminded of a Bolivian woman who roamed the Altaplano driving her llama herds day after day with little direction or purpose. It didn't matter too much which direction they wandered in. Then one day she was drawn into the gospel net, and her spirit responded to truth. When she learned of the mission of the Savior, the meaning of the atonement and His ultimate sacrifice, and the purpose of her earth life, she whispered, "You mean He did that for me?" And then, more as a testimony than a question, she repeated, "You mean He did that for me?" And He did, for you and for me. But if we are to claim our inheritance, we must each, individually, find Him.

Because of His atonement, through our obedience to gospel law we can find Him and become joint-heirs with Him in the fullness of our Father's kingdom. With this knowledge, what could possibly threaten or put in jeopardy our inheritance?

Agency plays a major part, for it is with our agency that

we cast our vote. And make no mistake, there are influences of an unseen enemy that seek relentlessly to entice us to what appear to be attractive alternatives and will lobby for our vote. Throughout the scriptures we read that Satan stirred up the hearts of people. "It is he who is the author of all sin. And behold, he doth carry on his works of darkness . . . from generation to generation according as he can get hold upon the hearts of the children of men." (Helaman 6:30.) We read that "the devil should tempt the children of men, or they could not be agents unto themselves; for if they never should have bitter they could not know the sweet." (D&C 29:39.)

President David O. McKay taught, "Your greatest weakness will be the point at which Satan will try to tempt you, will try to win you; and if you made yourself weak, he will add to that weakness." (*Improvement Era,* July 1968, p. 3.)

Our time is the time spoken of by the prophets, a time when the adversary is aggressively marshaling his forces as never before in the last great battle against righteousness. And he is using the same tactics as he employed in his attempts to distract the Savior from his appointed mission.

The first tactic is a temptation to appeal to the appetite, to an inherent craving to satisfy hunger and the demands of the flesh. An uncontrolled appetite attacks one's reasoning. It begins with rationalization, then justification, and finally the actual use of artificial stimulants, such as drugs and alcohol and pornography. When it gets out of hand, the result is personal devastation—not freedom, but enslavement. The question then is, Do I have an appetite for anything that could be enslaving?

The second tactic is to have us yield to pride, fashion, vanity, the praises of men, peer influence, and those things that separate us from the things of God. Our hearts become centered on the things of the world rather than the things of the spirit. Popularity, prestige, power, and positions become more important than humility, meekness, and teachability.

The third tactic is to gratify the hungering for the riches of the world. Is our ethical compass useful and visible and dependable? Can we say with Job, "Till I die I will not remove mine integrity from me"? (Job 27:5.) It is true that some people seem to have more temptations than others, and some have greater power of resistance than others. "But God is faithful, who will not suffer you to be tempted above that ye are able; but will with the temptation also make a way to escape, that ye may be able to bear it." (1 Corinthians 10:13.)

There could be no condemnation for our doing what we can't help, but we can help doing the things that violate the laws and commandments. God has given us power to resist these things, and we can call upon Him for strength that we lack. And by our habits, we gain control. It is our habits in relation to the gospel of Jesus Christ that bind us or free us. It is our habits that determine whether our inheritance is to be claimed or unclaimed. We are what we are because of our habits. The habit of striving to keep all of the commandments will change us from what we are to what we are to become. It is a process that changes our souls, our appetites, our desires. When we get the gospel on the inside and make it part of our very being, we have not just changed our habits; our habits have literally changed us, a mighty change.

We can have the gift of the Holy Ghost with us always, and that gift is more than a prompting to do right and wrong. As Elder Parley P. Pratt wrote, "It quickens all the intellectual faculties, increases, enlarges, expands, and purifies all the natural passions and affections. . . . It inspires virtue, kindness, goodness, tenderness, gentleness, and charity. It develops beauty of person, form, and features. It tends to health, vigor, animation, and social feeling. It invigorates all the faculties of the physical and intellectual man. It strengthens and gives tone to the nerves.

In short, it is, as it were, marrow to the bone, joy to the heart, light to the eyes, music to the ears, and life to the whole being. . . . Such is the gift of the Holy Ghost, and such are its operations when received through the lawful channel—the divine, eternal priesthood." (*Key to the Science of Theology* [Deseret Book, 1978 ed.], pp. 61–62.)

When we find ourselves out of control for a time, out of harmony, and disappointed in our actions in relation to our desires, we need not despair. There is a place of spiritual repair. We can take our wounded spirit faithfully and regularly to the sacrament altar and there renew our covenants, our commitments, by offering a broken heart and a contrite spirit. Then we begin, in part at least, to feel the healing, the peace, the deep, abiding love when we ponder the meaning of the atonement in our personal lives. There we will feel what Andrew and Nathaniel must have felt and say with them, "We have found the Christ. We have found Him. Come and see."

Some time ago I participated in a survival camp with a group of young people in the High Sierra Mountains. After three days of physically challenging and spiritually strengthening experiences, we faced one of the last activities—that of rappelling down an eighty-foot cliff.

When my turn came, I surveyed the setting. Overhead the sky was blue and clear. Over the edge of the cliff was a long, long way down, and I could not see the landing place below or the people who would welcome me or pick up the pieces. The instructor securely wrapped a strap around my legs and waist, placed the rappelling rope in my hand, and proceeded with instructions. It's fascinating how much better we listen and concentrate when we know that what is being said really matters. He had previously explained the skill of rappelling and the importance of the safety rope with each individual who went down the cliff ahead of me, but when it was my turn, I listened more intently. I wanted to know all that he knew. I didn't want any of the rules overlooked or minimized. If I followed the instructions, I'd get down safely; if not, I would suffer varying degrees of discomfort according to my ability to follow the instructions. I learned right away that his instructions were accurate when I experienced some discomforting rope burn on my hands.

Without looking down, but always looking up and straining to listen for instructions, advice, and encouragement, I began my descent. About halfway down, as I pondered my position, I was reminded of the teachings of President George Q. Cannon: "When we went forth into the waters of baptism and covenanted with our Father in heaven to serve Him and keep His commandments, He bound Himself also by covenant to us that He would never desert us, never leave us to ourselves, never forget us, that in the midst of trials and hardships, when everything was arrayed against us, He would be near unto us and would sustain us. That was His covenant." (*Gospel Truth*, 1987, p. 134.)

The Savior bound Himself to us. He is our safety rope. He throws out the lifeline—literally our lifeline. Through obedience to His laws and commandments, we tie ourselves securely to Him. The rope I held was the safety rope. I had my agency. I could hang on or I could let go. Or if I wanted, I could take out my pocket knife, exercise my agency, and cut just one fine strand at a time. Surely one strand at a time would present no risk.

I likened the rope to the commandments. I can break one commandment at a time. Surely one commandment at a time won't hurt. Would we ever consider letting go of a rope and challenging our ability to survive against the law of gravity? Or would we ignore the commandments of God and pit our resistance against the power of the adversary? If we choose to hold onto the rope, we are limited, restricted, curtailed, but through that very process our Father in heaven has said that He will make us free. Only after we are tried and tested can we be trusted with our inheritance as heirs to the kingdom of God. If we choose to let go of the rope and release ourselves from the laws and the commandments, we also choose the consequences, because even God obeys the law. Through disobedience to laws, we will fall.

Those men in prison, your brothers and mine, chose to let go of the rope. They cut themselves free of the laws and rejected the "hard sayings," and now within their prison walls they sing, "How gentle God's commands."

Let us each protect ourselves from enslavement and release ourselves from those prison walls of our own making, those things that weaken our grasp on the safety rope, the lifeline, the iron rod. The Savior taught that should one choose to willfully leave his parents and waste his inheritance in sin, his repentant return would be greeted with rejoicing and acceptance. Thus He illustrated the worth of souls to the Father and the love His disciples should have for each other.

Mary, the mother of Jesus, exemplified in the most glorious way her preparation and submission to the will of God when she responded to the angel Gabriel, "Behold the handmaid of the Lord; be it unto me according to thy word." (Luke 1:38.)

The Lord told his disciples, "Come, . . . follow me." (Matthew 19:21.) I know from my own experience that on those occasions when we follow with full purpose of heart, acting with integrity—no hypocrisy and no deception before God, but with all intent, repenting of our sins—we can feel that quiet assurance that we are free: free from the chains that bind, free from darkness and unbelief, free from depression and anger and hatred, free from jealousies and envy and cravings of the appetite, free from hungering for the riches of the world, free from fear and from error, free to claim our inheritance.

As we consider that day when the bishop called, "Chad, are you here?" and he came running, we can anticipate a similar day for each of us. Let us keep ever in our mind an anticipation of that glorious day when, with outstretched arms, our Father will greet us and we will respond, "Oh, my Father, I am home again." Then, if we are prepared, we will receive our inheritance and become the sons and daughters of God, heirs of God and joint-heirs with Jesus Christ.

Chapter 4

Choose to Return

Sometimes when we are discouraged, we may feel that life is too difficult. We are away from our heavenly home, and our spirits long to return. Have you ever walked alone in the evening and looked up at the stars and wondered, "What am I doing here? Where am I going? What is life all about?" It is good to think about these things, for if we don't think about them, we may not even understand the importance of the life we are living.

What was it like when we left home? We were the valiant ones, the faithful ones. We learned obedience there and chose to follow the Savior. We were given an opportunity to come to earth, and we came because we wanted to. We are here to be tried and tested. We are away from home on a mission, and God has given each of us our own divine mission.

When we made the transition from our heavenly home to this earth life, a veil was drawn over our eyes so we wouldn't remember what it was like there. We have to walk by faith. But sometimes we have deep spiritual feelings that assure us this isn't the beginning. Our Father told us that if we will exercise faith in Him, He will always be with us, and His Spirit will be with us to help us keep the commandments.

It is important for us to realize that in the battle that was waged in our pre-earth life, we chose to be on the

Lord's side. That same battle is continuing here on earth. It is a battle between right and wrong, good and evil, happiness and misery, freedom and enslavement. It is a battle between obedience and disobedience, light and darkness. It is a battle between being on the Lord's side or being on Satan's side. And we can choose.

When the Savior visited the American continent in the time of the Nephites, He told the people that He would come again. But He also warned them: "Ye must watch and pray always lest ye enter into temptation; for Satan desires to have you, that he may sift you as wheat." (3 Nephi 18:18.)

Yes, Satan desires to have us, and he will do everything in his power to persuade us to yield to his enticements. The battle between the followers of Satan and the followers of the Savior is now being waged, and for us to think casually about this great conflict is very dangerous. In fact, it can be life threatening. It can affect our very eternal life. The Lord warns us, "Whosoever perisheth, perisheth unto himself; and whosoever doeth iniquity, doeth it unto himself." He also tells us that the choice is ours: "For behold, ye are free; ye are permitted to act for yourselves. He hath given unto you that ye might know good from evil, and he hath given unto you that ye might choose life or death; and ye can do good and be restored unto that which is good, or have that which is good restored unto you; or ye can do evil, and have that which is evil restored unto you." (Helaman 14:30–31.)

We have our agency and can make our own choices. But we cannot blame anyone else for the choices we make. We are each responsible for our own actions. That being the case, how can we be sure that we will return home from our earthly mission when we have so many decisions to make each day?

To guide us, we have scriptures, the blessing of daily prayer, and a living prophet. When I listen to general conference and our prophet tells us what we should do and encourages us to do it, I think he is telling us because he knows the lessons that we need to learn before we get back home. He knows what is at stake. We need to listen to the promptings of the Spirit and to know that when our prophet speaks, he is speaking to each of us.

We are each in control of our own life. If we are successful, it isn't because of luck. Success comes through hard work, commitment, and strenuous effort, and through the grace of God. In the Book of Mormon we read, "Therefore, cheer up your hearts, and remember that ye are free to act for yourselves—to choose the way of everlasting death or the way of eternal life. Wherefore, . . . reconcile yourselves to the will of God, and not to the will of the devil and the flesh; and remember, after ye are reconciled unto God, that it is only in and through the grace of God that ye are saved." (2 Nephi 10:23–24.)

When I was a child, I remember saying, "Dad, can I do such and such?" And my father would say, "Suit yourself, but I wouldn't." In a way, that is what our Heavenly Father is saying. He gives us the plan and says this is what He wants us to do, but we have our agency. We are responsible for the choices we make and must live with the consequences of those choices.

Sometimes it might be easier if our Father would tell us, "No, I'm going to make you do what you should do." Why doesn't He do that? Because that was Satan's plan. We didn't vote for that plan, because it would have meant that we wouldn't be able to grow and become all that we can be. Does that mean we're not going to make any mistakes? No. We are going to make lots of mistakes, and our Father in heaven knew we would and that we could learn and grow because of them. A mistake can either destroy or refine us, and it isn't a total mistake if we learn from it.

On one occasion as a child, I had a difficult choice to make. I came home from school much later than I was supposed to, and my father was waiting for me. I was raised on a farm, and he was coming around the corner of the chicken coop when he saw me. He said, "Come over here and sit down," motioning to a log. That wasn't the first time I had come home late. My father and I often sat close together on the log and talked, but that day I sat on the end of the log, as far away as I could get. He said to me, "Ardie, I'm going to have to help you to learn obedience and responsibility, to be where you're supposed to be." Then I noticed he had a green willow in his hand. Stroking the willow, he said, "I'm going to give you your choice. You can stay home for a week or you can have a licking."

I didn't like either of those choices. The licking would last a shorter time, but the suffering would be more intense. That was the first time I remember being faced with a really hard choice to make, and I remember struggling with it. Should I take the licking or should I stay home for a week? And how could I avoid such hard choices in the future? It was then that the concept of obedience began to formulate in my mind.

Since then I have had to make many choices in my life, most of them much harder than that one. We are told that we will be tried and tested, and it isn't intended to be easy. Each of us has many trials and is tried many times. And for each of us, our tests will be where we are the weakest. That is where Satan will tempt us. Your tests are different from mine. The things that are the hardest for me are where I am being tested, just as the things that are the hardest for you are where you are being tested. We must be on guard at all times against all temptations, for Satan desires to have us, to enslave us and destroy us.

When I was a student at Brigham Young University many years ago, I left my wallet in the telephone booth at the Joseph Smith Building. There was ten dollars in it, all the money I had. I went to the BYU lost-and-found department, but the wallet had not been turned in.

Nine years later I received a letter in the mail that had been routed through a clinic in Calgary, Alberta, where I had had a physical examination several years before. The letter had been sent to the clinic, which had forwarded it to my parents in Canada, and they in turn had sent it on to me. I opened the envelope and read the following message: "To Whom It May Concern. Anyone knowing the whereabouts of Ardeth Greene please forward this letter. It is very important that contact be made as soon as possible to settle some unfinished business at the B.Y.U." The return address was in Salt Lake City, where I was then living, so I called the sender immediately because I wanted to know what the unfinished business could be.

When I identified myself on the telephone, a quiet voice said, "I'm so glad to hear from you." Then she told me this story: "I was a student at BYU nine years ago and I had no money. My parents had no money, and I needed ten dollars to complete my registration fee. I borrowed ten dollars from my boyfriend, and I promised I'd pay him back Friday. Then I prayed fervently that I would somehow be able to get the money to repay the debt. That day I went into a telephone booth on campus and there was a wallet. I opened the wallet and there was a ten-dollar bill."

How would you have reacted in that situation? Would you have thought that finding the wallet was an answer to prayer? What would Satan want you to think? Do you think that young woman thought about being tempted at that moment? Remember, she wasn't being tempted with cigarettes or alcohol or whatever else. She was tempted because of the urgent need for ten dollars.

She continued her report. "I took the ten dollars and returned the money to my boyfriend. For all these nine years, I've had that wallet in my top dresser drawer. Every time I clean I want to throw it away, but you know you can't make a wrong right by throwing it away. You have to make it right by doing right." Several years later she looked through the wallet one more time, and this time she noticed a little card she had not seen before. The name of the clinic in Calgary was on that card.

On the phone she said, "Oh, I'll be so happy to return this wallet to you." I was working at the telephone company at the time, so I suggested, "Would you bring it into the office?" She said, "Oh, I'd be too embarrassed. I've never stolen anything before or since, and I'm really embarrassed." I replied, "I'd be honored to meet someone as honest as you." Yes, she had made a mistake, but was she a bad person? No. She was a good person, and she had gone to great lengths to make things right. Finally she agreed to come to my office.

When I came back from lunch one day, a beautiful young woman was waiting for me. I walked over and sat across from her, and she laid the wallet on the desk. Looking directly at me, she said, "I hope this means as much to you now as it did to me the day I took it." I reached for her hand and said, "I consider it such a great privilege to meet such an honest and noble person." She smiled and said, "This is so good. This problem has hung like a millstone around my neck for nine years, and now I've set it right." After she left, I went to the window and watched her go down the sidewalk with a skip in her step.

We all make mistakes, but there are ways to set things right. Sometimes it's a lot harder than just returning a wallet after nine years, but there's always a way to set something right. There's always a way back. The little "termites" that eat away inside us don't need to destroy us. But we must recognize them and get rid of them before they become destructive and destroy this tabernacle of flesh and this spirit that's eternal. We can't afford to let even little termites, our little sins, go unresolved. They can destroy us.

Once when I was speaking to a group about the importance of doing what's right and the seriousness of mistakes, I saw a young woman in the back of the hall get up and walk out. I felt sick about it. I wanted to shout, "Come back. Please come back." Then I noticed another young woman get up and walk out, and that made me feel even worse.

Later I learned that the second person was the Laurel class president. She had seen the other Laurel, for whom she had a responsibility, get up and leave, and knowing that the girl was having some problems in her life, she went after her to try to bring her back. She couldn't get the girl to come back in, but after the meeting she came to me and said, "Will you go talk to my friend? She needs help." I said, "Of course I will." And I wanted to add, "There's always a way back. Come back. Come back."

Yes, there *is* a way back. All of the Father's blessings are intended for us if we will just choose to be obedient. And when we make mistakes, He understands and He will forgive if we put things right. Satan would have us think, "Look, you've made a serious mistake. You might as well give up. There's no way back." But there *is* a way back. That is the message of the gospel. That is the glad tidings. Sometimes the way is difficult and painful and takes a long, long time, but there is a way back.

The first principle of the gospel is faith in the Lord Jesus Christ. This means that we must come to know our Savior—to know that He really exists and that He knows us. It means coming to know that He loved us so much that He gave His life for us. It means knowing that we can make it back home because He has provided a way. Through faith in the atonement of Jesus Christ and repentance of sin, by the grace of God we can receive eternal life and exaltation after we have expended our own best efforts.

Some time ago I received a letter from a young woman I had met several months earlier while on an overseas assignment. She told me of a serious mistake she had made and added, "And now, for some reason, I don't pray anymore. It's hard for me to pray. I can't read the Book of Mormon anymore. I feel like I'm caught in a trap and I can't get out. I don't have a testimony, but I want one." At the end of the letter, she pleaded, "Please help."

Was there anything I could do for her? Was it too late?

Let me tell you of a rescue that took place. A number of years ago, at 4:45 on a Friday afternoon in April, radio and television news commentators put aside international news to headline the story of a desperate rescue attempt. A child had fallen into a deep abandoned well. Within half an hour firemen were pumping oxygen into a small opening in the shaft. A rope was lowered into a darkened hole and anxious voices were shouting, "Try to grab hold of the rope, Kathy. Grab hold of the rope." In response they heard this weak response: "I am. I am." And then the voice ceased. Efforts to raise Kathy with a rope had failed.

That night under a blaze of lights, men and machines worked feverishly to try to rescue the child. Hundreds of people volunteered. Circus midgets in the vicinity came and risked their lives trying to get through the narrow shaft. Exhausted rescuers faced great danger as they worked through layers of rock. One report told of men on a ship at sea who listened to the reports and took up a collection of money in their desire to help. It was reported that seldom had so much prayer power been focused on one person or on one rescue. And under all these great machines, bright lights, and loudspeakers lay a tiny girl. What about her? Was there water where she lay? Was she conscious? Was she still alive? And what about her parents, who waited anxiously, not knowing what the outcome would be?

After the total expenditure of half a million dollars and fifty-three hours of rescue efforts, the trapped girl's doctor went down into the tunnel and the answer came: Kathy Fiscus, the little girl whom the world had come to know and love, was dead. She had apparently died shortly after she had last spoken. While so many millions mourned the tragedy of little Kathy, they didn't realize that Kathy was all right. She had gone back home. Maybe she had gone early, but she had returned.

This is not the kind of rescue that we are most concerned about. We are not so concerned about the body.

Spiritual rescues are the kind we must strive for. When I received the letter from the young girl who was crying for help, I wanted to get on a plane and go to her and shout, "Try to grab hold of the rope!" But I would have said, "Grab hold of the iron rod. Hang on. You can make it. I know you can. We all can make it if we choose to. Our Elder Brother made it possible."

I often wonder how the Savior would feel if, having given His life for us so that we can make it back home, He were to hear us say, "Yes, you gave your life for me, but I didn't choose to be obedient to the laws and ordinances of the gospel. I cannot qualify for the promised blessings. So in my case, you gave your life in vain."

It cannot be that way. One day we must come to realize that He gave his life for us. And because He did so, we can set things right insofar as possible, for He has made up the difference. The prophets have taught that there won't ever be a greater test than the test that we are experiencing here in this earth life. The challenge lies in having opposition in all things and then being allowed to act for ourselves. (See 2 Nephi 2:16.)

Now I don't know about your choices, but I do know about mine, and there are some things that I want to do better than I have done before. And maybe there are some important adjustments that each of us need to make in order to follow the path. We need to reach out to each other and be part of the rescue team. We need to shout to everyone who needs our help, "Come back! Come back if you've made mistakes!" We must open our circle large enough to include everyone, and hold to the iron rod.

I know that our Savior lives and cares about us. Whatever He asks of us, is it too much? Surely it's not enough to pay the price in return for what He has done for us. Let us choose to return.

Chapter 5

My Sister, My Friend

My sister, my friend, I wish it were possible to say to you, "Come into my home. Sit on my hearth. Let's talk." If we were just sitting together, you and I, we could share things that are important in a more personal way. I would want you to know of my assurance of God's love for each of us.

And you would share your thoughts with me. "And do you know this? And have you read this? And look how this relates to that." We would turn to our scriptures and discover together. So let us imagine in our minds that we are sitting side by side together, close enough to say to each other, "This is how it feels inside my heart."

When my husband and I travel together in the car, often it will be quiet for a minute, then one will say to the other, "What's on your mind? What are you thinking?" Then we ramble on and on. Maybe there isn't a lot of correlation in all that is said, but when it is all over, we feel right. So, will you ramble with me for a minute?

Let's begin with a statement from President Spencer W. Kimball, who said that we women are to be scholars of the scriptures. Why? I think that one of the reasons is that words form our thoughts, and our thoughts control our feelings, and our feelings control our actions. That is an exciting thing to discover. Then I would probably pull out my file and say to you, my sister, "Do you know what

Hugh Nibley has said about that?" And we would share this thought from him:

"We can think only one thing at a time. We hold thousands of instantaneous impressions in suspension, just long enough to make our choices and drop those we don't want. Why the mind chooses to focus on one object to the exclusion of all others remains a mystery. But one thing is clear, the blocked out signals are the unwanted ones, and the ones we favor are our deliberate choice. I can think anything I want to, absolutely anything with this provision. Then when I choose to focus my attention on one subject, all other subjects are dropped into the background. We are always thinking something, selecting what will fit into the world we are making for ourselves."

Related to this idea is this scripture from the Book of Mormon: "Then cometh the judgment of the Holy One . . . the time that he that is filthy shall be filthy still; and he that is righteous shall be righteous still; he that is happy shall be happy still; and he that is unhappy shall be unhappy still." (Mormon 9:14.)

We'd talk about this scripture. "You mean I'm not going to move from here to there and find it's all wonderful? And if I'm not happy here, do you mean that I won't be happy there? Is that what it means?" I think it is. But how do we find happiness here in the midst of trials?

Psychologist Victor Frankl says, "Suffering isn't suffering the minute that we find a reason for it." If we understand the purpose in suffering, we can learn from it and can become stronger because of it. Our Savior set the pattern. We read in the scriptures, "Though he were a Son, yet learned he obedience by the things which he suffered." (Hebrews 5:8.) Instead of thinking, "Why me? It isn't fair," we consider what we might learn from the experience and what God would have us do. It is when we learn to seek, ask, and knock that we find Him.

Then we would turn to the Doctrine and Covenants and

read: "My people must be tried in all things, that they may be prepared to receive the glory that I have for them, even the glory of Zion." (D&C 136:31.) We must be tried in all things: spiritually, physically, emotionally, socially, mentally. This being the case, if we are not having any trials, maybe we ought to pray for a few. Of course, no one is going to pray for more tests, but we can pray for the strength to be faithful and endure to the end.

We are not going to be tested beyond that which we can handle. The Lord knows us. We may think we've gone as far as we can, but He will push us a little farther. Another favorite scripture of mine is found in Second Corinthians, when Paul talks to Timothy about comforting each other. He says, "Blessed be God, . . . who comforteth us in all our tribulation, that we may be able to comfort them which are in any trouble, by the comfort wherewith we ourselves are comforted of God. For . . . as [we] are partakers of the sufferings, so shall [we] be also of the consolation." (2 Corinthians 1:3–4, 7.)

In the book of Ether, Moroni says: "I would show unto the world that faith is things which are hoped for and not seen; wherefore, dispute not because ye see not, for ye receive no witness until after the trial of your faith." (Ether 12:6.) I don't know if our trials will last a week, a month, a year, or a lifetime, but I do know that each of us has a mission. Each of us has a purpose. It is in coming to know the Lord's will that we can feel peace in times of tribulation. It is, in fact, while we are struggling that we can come to know the Lord—not just read about Him, not just know His will, but know *Him.* He will speak to our minds and we will hear and know.

We may sometimes think that it is too difficult, too much for us to bear. Then we realize that we are not alone. The Lord has told us, "I will go before your face. I will be on your right hand and on your left, and my Spirit shall be in your hearts, and mine angels round about you, to bear you up." (D&C 84:88.) On the other side are those who are near and dear to us, and sometimes they can seem very close to us. I bear testimony of this. Those who know our needs and wants, I believe, are privileged sometimes in the quiet of our solitude to impress things upon our minds that help us to understand.

I was struggling one time in the quiet of my solitude when my father's voice came into my mind and said, "My dear, don't worry about the little things and the big things that you agreed to before you came."

When we have plateaus and feel as if we are not growing, or when we fall short of what we wish we were, I think of what President George Q. Cannon said:

"It is true that some have greater power of resistance than others, but everyone has the power to close his heart against doubt, against darkness, against unbelief, against depression, against anger, against hatred, against jealousy, against malice, against envy. God has given this power unto all of us, and we can gain still greater power by calling upon Him for that which we lack. If it were not so, how could we be condemned for giving way to wrong influences? . . .

"God has given us power to resist these things, that our hearts may be kept free from them and also from doubt; and when Satan comes and assails us, it is our privilege to say, 'Get thee behind me, Satan, for I have no lot nor portion in you, and you have no part in me. I am in the service of my God or about the work of God, and I will not listen to you.' " (*Gospel Truth*, 1987, pp. 16, 17.)

Understanding the gospel provides strength within, and we come to find out better than ever before who we really are. I believe that when we come to know who we are, we don't suffer feelings of inadequacy. We are painfully aware of our shortcomings, but they don't immobilize us. They help us to focus our efforts and overcome our weaknesses.

How do we take the steps that move us off the plateau we are on to a higher level of spirituality? This occurs when we experience a real need, a real want, a desire akin to thirst. This may be experienced in a variety of ways.

For example, how many testimonies have you seen borne out of the anguish of people suffering with serious physical problems? One evening my ward Relief Society president, who at the time was suffering with cancer, called me on the phone and said, "I know you've been busy this week. What time would you like me to bring your supper over to you?" While her body was raging with cancer, her spirit was reaching out to others, her faith was strong and unwavering, and her example strengthened the faith of her family and friends. Sometimes sickness is necessary for our spiritual growth.

Our testimonies may also be strengthened when we lose someone who is very near and dear to us. At such a time, the other side seems so close. When our loved ones are there, and we know they are there, the other side seems much more a reality, our testimonies are strengthened, and we begin to look forward, not to make us homesick, but at least to live with anticipation of one day going home.

Finally, if it isn't death, it might be floods or earthquakes or something beyond our ability to control that turns us toward our Father. We learn to listen as we have never listened before, and we learn to trust.

In the past few months, I've come to know the Lord's will on things that I have yearned to know for a lifetime. My testimony is that this has happened because I have searched more diligently, I have listened more intently, and I have needed to know more desperately. He is there. We can hear. We need not be perfect vessels. He will speak to imperfect vessels according to our diligence and according to our faith.

As you sit at my hearth and we are sharing some thoughts, I would share with you just two or three things that I feel are essential. First, have faith. We need to have faith in the Lord Jesus Christ. We need to know in our hearts, and if we don't know, we need to ask.

One time when I was feeling far away, but realizing that it is never the Lord who puts the distance between us, but the distractions that we let creep into our hearts and that lead us away from instead of toward the light, I asked the question, Where do we go for comfort, for higher spiritual ground? And now I have the answer, at least in part. I go to the scriptures. The Lord will speak to me. Often He will answer my prayers through the scriptures. As I read, I may think, *I never saw that scripture before. That was written for me.* Then I will write the date in the margin and that scripture becomes mine.

One scripture that is for me—and for you also—tells us: "Draw near unto me and I will draw near unto you; seek me diligently and ye shall find me; ask, and ye shall receive; knock, and it shall be opened unto you. . . . And if your eye be single to my glory, your whole [body] shall be filled with light, and there shall be no darkness [no depression, no despondency, no discouragement] in you; and that body which is filled with light comprehendeth all things. Therefore, sanctify yourselves that your minds become single to God, and the days will come that you shall see him; for he will unveil his face unto you, and it shall be in his own time, and in his own way, and according to his own will." (D&C 88:63, 67–68.)

Do we believe this? I know we do! But do we practice it? Do we ask? I see increasingly the evidence that the Lord does hear and does answer our prayers. So I would say, have faith.

Second, I would say, know of your divine nature. Know who you really are. Sometimes I think we suffer because we don't really know who we are. I like what President George Q. Cannon has said: "We are the children of God, and as His children there is no attribute we ascribe to Him that we do not possess, though they may be dormant or in embryo." (*Gospel Truth,* 1987, p. 3.)

Do you ever get up in the morning and look in the mirror and say, "Ho hum. You and me throughout all eternity"? Look deeper into your heart and soul. See yourself as a daughter of God. Try to look beyond the flesh. You are endowed and blessed with a pure spirit struggling to overcome the weaknesses of the flesh.

Each of us came to earth with a pure spirit. Sometimes one's spirit is wounded because the demands of the flesh overtake the spirit. What do we do then? Do we give up or give out or give in? No. We come to the sacrament table with a contrite heart and a broken spirit. We partake of sacred emblems. Those emblems are not changed into the body and the flesh, as some theologians teach. The change takes place inside the soul of the person who partakes. Then we can start again—and again—because we know the Lord loves us unconditionally. We never walk alone.

Let us each feel the responsibility to grow spiritually so that we are different today than we were last year. If we are just the same this year as we were last year, we may not live fifty years, but just live the same year fifty times. This year must be different from last year; otherwise life can become routine and even boring, without growth, and our mission will never be realized.

We don't want life to be overwhelming as a result of trying to run faster than we should, but we don't want it to be underwhelming either. It is all right to get tired, but never bored. We need never to get tired of life so long as we have so much to learn.

With a testimony that is undeniable, I know that God hears our prayers. He knows our needs. He will allow us to suffer, and from that suffering can come great spiritual growth. One day as we look back, we will be grateful for the times we tried and made it. We will be grateful for prayers delayed but not unanswered. We will come to know the mysteries of God and be grateful for the tests, all of them.

I love to read these words of Nephi: "And I, Nephi, did go unto the mount oft, and I did pray oft unto the Lord; wherefore the Lord showed unto me great things."

(1 Nephi 18:3.) I would trade my degrees from two universities for the things that I have come to know in going to the mountain. That mountain need not be literally a mountain. It can be in the privacy of our own home. It is usually in the morning for me, before the activities of the day begin.

We can know the things we need to know to fulfill our mission. I am sure of that. In the Doctrine and Covenants we read: "Teach ye diligently and my grace shall attend you, that you may be instructed more perfectly . . . in doctrine, in the law of the gospel, in all things that pertain to the kingdom of God, that are expedient for you to understand." (D&C 88:78.) That is fascinating to me. It is as we teach each other that we learn.

When I hear sisters say, "I don't want to teach the young women. I don't want to teach the Primary. I need to be in Relief Society," I want to say, "For precious little time will only a few be selected to teach the children and to teach the young women. It is in teaching diligently that we are instructed more perfectly." Those who are privileged to have a calling to teach the children for a short time can enhance and hasten their spiritual understanding as they are teaching, not just as they are being taught.

As I think about the things that put us on higher ground spiritually, I think of the opportunity to serve. President Marion G. Romney said, "The Lord sends us to minister to one another. Obtaining a remission of our sins comes from caring for one another. The efficacy of our prayers depends on how we care for one another." How much do we care for one another? We'll take a loaf of bread, we'll make a phone call. But when we serve, something also needs to happen inside the soul. I call that soul service. It is through service that we experience a level of spirituality that lifts us higher than we otherwise might ever attain.

If we will radiate the truth that we know because of the faith that is born in us, out of struggles, out of hurts, out of disappointments, but also out of faith and out of knowledge of the Lord's love for us, He will speak His mind and will to us and we can stand as witnesses of God at all times, in all things, and in all places. And we will qualify for eternal life.

May we go forth in the coming years on a higher plateau spiritually than we have ever known before as daughters of light spreading joy and happiness wherever we go, through faith in the Lord Jesus Christ.

Part II

The Journey

Chapter 6

Here I Am, but Where Am I Going?

When Adam left Eden, he left on a question, "Adam, where art thou?" Did God not know where Adam was? Actually He is the only one who does know. If we were to be asked that question, we might answer, I am here, but where is here? And more important, where am I going, not geographically but spiritually?

President David O. McKay defined spirituality as "our true aim, . . . the consciousness of victory over self and of communion with the infinite." (*Stepping Stones to an Abundant Life* [Deseret Book, 1971], p. 99.) The scriptures tell us that the spirit and the body are the soul of man. (See D&C 88:15.) If we are to have consciousness of victory over self, we must make the demands of the flesh submissive to the spirit. President Spencer W. Kimball taught that God "wants us to perfect ourselves and maintain control of ourselves. He does not want Satan and others to control our lives." (*Ensign*, October 1982, p. 2.)

We must learn that keeping our Heavenly Father's commandments represents the only path to total control of ourselves, the only way to find joy, truth, and fulfillment in this life and in eternity. Spirituality, victory over self, impels us to conquer difficulties and acquire strength, which I believe means self-control, as we face the challenges of life.

From childhood we learn to face physical challenges,

then move on to social challenges, then emotional challenges, and finally spiritual growth. For each of us, our experiences are varied, but the lessons we learn have many similarities. The very purpose of this life is that we might be tested and gradually gain control and self-mastery as we learn to obey all our Father's laws and come to know Him and His Son, Jesus Christ.

Knowing God in the ultimate and full sense can allow us to think what He would think, say what He would say, do what He would do, and be like Him in character, in attributes, and ultimately in perfection. He can become the very center of our lives until we experience an unfolding of our faculties, an expanding of our souls, and an awakening of the spirit within us. To know Him is to have His will constantly in our minds, in our thoughts, in our actions, in the resolution of our differences, in our decisions, in our responses, in our interpretations—indeed, in our total experience in life. Through oneness with Him, we begin to understand our reason for being, and those trials and problems that we might otherwise choose to avoid may become the very foundation that brings us to the threshold of spirituality.

At this point, as never before, we begin to have a plan for our life. Rather than asking, "What do we want to have happen?" we ask, "What does He want to have happen?" Then each day we begin to really live and to savor every moment of life with new insight and understanding, with purpose and reason, following a plan that gives direction. This is more than setting goals. It is a pattern and a plan that allow us not only to set goals but to reach them because of a higher motivation. We move from the struggle—the battle of trying to control ourselves with will power and overcoming temptation—until we have a mighty change of heart. We no longer need will power because our will is His will.

And with this mighty change of heart, we have no more disposition to do evil, but want to do good continually. We are free from the battle fatigue of this life because we have yielded our hearts to God through the process of the mighty change. Every day of life is a precious gift.

When I consider how precious this life can be, I am reminded of Thornton Wilder's play *Our Town*. One of the main characters is a young woman, Emily, who dies and discovers that she has the opportunity to live one day of her life over again. She chooses her twelfth birthday. When the day begins, her first reaction is an intense desire to savor every moment. "I can't look at everything hard enough," she says. Then to her sorrow she sees that the members of her family are not experiencing life with any intensity. In desperation she says, "Let's look at one another." And then she says, "I can't. I can't go on. It goes so fast. We don't have time to look at one another. I didn't realize. So all that was going on, and we never noticed. Take me back—up the hill—to my grave. But first: Wait! One more look. Good-by, world. Good-by, Grover's Corners, . . . Mama and Papa. Good-by to clocks ticking, . . . and Mama's sunflowers. And food and coffee. And new-ironed dresses and hot baths . . . and sleeping and waking up. Oh, earth, you're too wonderful for anybody to realize you. Do any human beings ever realize life while they live it?—every, every minute?" The narrator, or stage manager, replies, "No." He pauses and then adds, "The saints and poets, maybe—they do some."

Oh, if we could just talk to all of the Emilys and, yes, saints and poets and Latter-day Saints! If we could just help everyone to know that with that inner control which brings communion with the infinite, all of life can be a constant revelation, and that we can begin to see it, to live it, and to experience each moment! Even difficult experiences, stresses, and strain can provide insight and an unfolding if we could actually understand what is happening to us and consider what we can learn from the situations in which we find ourselves. As we come to know who we are, what our purpose in life is, and what our relationship with the

Savior is, we begin to develop inner control and victory over self. We begin to understand that we are the children of God, and that as His children, we can become like Him.

We didn't come to earth to gain spirituality. We brought it with us. Our task is to practice it through self-mastery, self-discipline, and communion with God in prayer and scripture study. Nephi taught, "Angels speak by the power of the Holy Ghost; wherefore, they speak the words of Christ. Wherefore, I said unto you, feast upon the words of Christ; for behold the words of Christ will tell you all things what ye should do. . . . For if ye would hearken unto the Spirit which teacheth a man to pray ye would know that ye must pray. . . . I say unto you that ye must pray always, and not faint; that ye must not perform any thing unto the Lord save in the first place ye shall pray unto the Father in the name of Christ." (2 Nephi 32:3, 8–9.)

The heavens are not closed to us unless we ourselves close them. We should expect communication with our Father in heaven. The Prophet Joseph Smith, speaking of revelation, said, "A person may profit by noticing the first intimation of the spirit of revelation; for instance, when you feel pure intelligence flowing into you, it may give you sudden strokes of ideas, so that by noticing it, you may find it fulfilled the same day or soon; (i.e.) those things that were presented unto your minds by the Spirit of God, will come to pass; and thus by learning the Spirit of God and understanding it, you may grow into the principle of revelation, until you become perfect in Jesus Christ." (*Teachings of the Prophet Joseph Smith* [Deseret Book, 1976], p. 151.)

In communion with the Lord, there are those times when we know with certainty that He is with us. This can happen as it did when the apostles were traveling on the road to Emmaus and said one to another, "Did not our heart burn within us, while he talked with us by the way, and while he opened to us the scriptures?" (Luke 24:32.)

Some time ago in Monterrey, Mexico, a sister and I walked along a dirt path shaded by olive trees. We were on the Lord's errand, traveling together to visit a sister in a remote area. Initially I felt some reservation about this assignment because I didn't know the people, didn't know the language, didn't know the culture, and didn't know exactly what to say. But as we walked together in the quiet of that morning, I contemplated the possibility of our having the Lord with us, as a companion. And while we did not see Him, I did witness a burning within, an excitement, an assurance, a witness of the Spirit that He walked with us on our way, which was His way. I have found that communion with the infinite most often occurs when we are in the act of serving someone else.

There are times when we may feel our service is of considerably less consequence than that of others whose contributions seem more visible, more magnificent, more far-reaching, and much more generous because of skills, finances, abilities, or self-confidence. On those occasions when I feel that my contribution is of infinitesimal proportion, I think of that great occasion when Jesus stood before the multitude, with evening approaching. The disciples suggested that it was time for the people to go into the village to get food. But Jesus said, "They need not depart." (Matthew 14:16.) One of the disciples found a young boy who had five loaves and two fish. The possibility of feeding five thousand people with just five loaves of bread and two fish must have seemed quite absurd. In fact, I can almost hear the young boy saying, "You want my lunch to feed five thousand?" But the message for me is that he gave all that he had, his five loaves and two fish.

We read that the Lord, after commanding the multitude to sit down on the grass, took the five loaves and two fish and gave thanks and blessed the food. Then he gave the loaves to his disciples to distribute to the multitude, and everyone ate and was filled. Afterwards the disciples picked up the fragments that remained and filled twelve baskets. (See John 6:5–13.)

When we give all that we have, the Lord will take it and bless it and magnify it and pass it, and there will be enough and to spare. It is only when we withhold what we have that we deprive ourselves of the promised blessing of grace, which our Bible Dictionary defines as "an enabling power that allows men and women to lay hold on eternal life and exaltation after they have expended their own best efforts." When we do our best, it is enough, and the Lord will make up the difference.

I have had experiences, as I am sure you have, that give me reason to know that as we begin to gain victory over ourselves and commune with the infinite, we can experience spirituality every day. I arose very early one day and, glancing out the window, witnessed in a reverent and different way the dawning of a new day. The sky was turning a delicate pink, in contrast to the deep green hills. I walked out on the balcony to better experience the manifestations of God's creations. The light and shadows changed quickly and quietly, and I felt that I had literally experienced the birth of a new day in the great eternal plan.

While pondering that experience, I thought of the conversation between Korihor and Alma in the Book of Mormon. "And now Korihor said unto Alma: If thou wilt show me a sign, that I may be convinced that there is a God, yea, show unto me that he hath power, and then will I be convinced of the truth of thy words. But Alma said unto him: Thou hast had signs enough; will ye tempt your God? Will ye say, Show unto me a sign, when ye have the testimony of all these thy brethren, and also all the holy prophets? The scriptures are laid before thee, yea, and all things denote there is a God; yea, even the earth, and all things that are upon the face of it, yea, and its motion, and also all the planets which move in their regular form do witness that there is a Supreme Creator." (Alma 30:43–44.) Spiritual manifestations are all around us, but too frequently we fail to drink them in.

As we strive for communion with the infinite, we are much like the men in a story told by William George Jordan. During a violent storm their ship was driven far off course and carried into a strange bay. Though their water supply was gone and they suffered the agony of thirst, the crew dared not drink the salt water of the sea. Finally, in desperation they lowered a bucket over the ship's side and drank what they thought was seawater, but to their amazement the water was fresh and life-giving. They were in a fresh-water arm of the sea, and they had only to reach down and accept the new life and strength for which they craved.

And so it is with us. We are surrounded by things that might strengthen us spiritually if we would just drop down our bucket. If we could always be in tune with the Spirit and the whisperings of the Spirit, we would learn to pay attention and give heed to the wealth of resources all around us.

In life we are constantly faced with ruts, distractions, barriers, and sometimes seemingly insurmountable obstacles. For some it may be the searching for the very purpose of this life, a reason for being. For others it is the sorting out of voices of the world that sound reasonable but are not compatible with an inner sense, causing our minds and our hearts to get out of harmony with each other. For some it may be time schedules and physical exhaustion.

One of the barriers has to do with a different kind of timing. We all want things to happen according to our own predetermined time schedule. When events are out of sequence with our natural desires, we may become distracted and frustrated. We fail to realize that with delay may come increased opportunity for preparation.

I have some feeling for this kind of distraction, this

enemy to spirituality. According to the yearnings of my heart and soul and my seemingly righteous desires, I had programmed my life to include a large family, to be a mother and a grandmother, the mother of a missionary, the mother of a bride, and on and on. But not so. The Lord's timeline for me was different. And what for a long time appeared to me to be a tragedy became the very foundation for deep spirituality. It is in matters of great consequence that we reach and touch divinity. And so I have learned that the exact time schedule for an event in one's life is not the real issue. The issue is not when a thing will happen, but the intensity of the preparation, the inner peace, the trust, the communion with the infinite, until it happens.

Elder Neal A. Maxwell, speaking of our individual timeline, has said, "The Lord will customize the curriculum for us in order to teach us the things we most need to know. He will set before us in life what we need, not always what we like. What therefore may seem now to be mere unconnected pieces of tile will someday, when we look back, take form and pattern and we will realize that God was making a mosaic."

After much pondering and years of reaching, I finally came to know that inner peace which brings increased power to communicate. The answer is in the scriptures: "Trust in the Lord with all thine heart; and lean not unto thine own understanding. In all thy ways acknowledge him, and he shall direct thy paths." (Proverbs 3:5–6.) Through certain knowledge of this counsel and implicit trust in our Father in heaven and the Savior, we can live on a higher spiritual plain.

For some of us, a barrier to spirituality is that we fail to systematically pursue the requirements for spiritual powers. This quest requires quiet time in a personal relationship—alone, yet not alone—where we find answers to things the world doesn't know, and where we inquire and come to know for ourselves. During this quiet time we tell the Lord how it is with us, review our promises and covenants in private, hold a "stewardship interview" concerning our lives up to this time, ponder the words of the Lord for increased understanding, and, on occasion, experience an unfolding—an awakening, as it were—of things we have known before, sometimes referred to as "divine echoes."

After meditation comes a time of resolve and commitment, mentally and spiritually, through self-discipline and self-mastery. Then, through prayer, we can humble ourselves and cleanse the inner vessel by praying mightily for forgiveness. When this pouring out of our heart and soul is accompanied by periods of fasting, though we may not always recognize the answer, we can experience inner peace while we await further direction.

Another barrier to spirituality—and perhaps the most common and the most powerful, and certainly the most persistent—is the power of the evil one. President George Q. Cannon stated: "If we could see with our spiritual senses as we now see with our natural senses, we should be greatly shocked at the sight of the influences that prompt us to disobey the counsels of God or the Spirit of the Lord in our hearts." (*Gospel Truth*, 1987, p. 65.)

President Spencer W. Kimball observed, "I find that when I get casual in my relationship with divinity and when it seems that no divine ear is listening and no divine voice is speaking, that I am far, far away, if I immerse myself in the scriptures, the distance narrows and the spirituality returns." (*The Teachings of Spencer W. Kimball* [Bookcraft, 1982], p. 135.)

And so we acknowledge that there are many barriers to our spirituality. The war in heaven continues. Someday the war will be won and there will be an eventual triumph of the forces of Christ over those of Satan, a permanent victory. But for here and now, the battle wages. As we increase in spirituality, we can have the Holy Spirit to be with us always, and then we will find ourselves in God's service, reaching out to others.

I like the words of Mother Teresa, the Catholic nun who has devoted her life to serving the poor in India: "We must not drift away from the humble works because these are the works nobody will do. It is never too small. We are so small, we look at things in a small way, but God, being almighty, sees everything great. Therefore even if you write a letter for a blind man or you just go and sit and listen or you take the mail for him or you visit somebody or bring a flower to somebody, small things, or wash clothes for somebody, or clean the house, very humble work, that is where you and I must be. For there are many people who can do big things, but there are very few people who will do the small things. Our loaves and our fishes can feed thousands.

"Give Jesus not only your hands to serve, but your heart to love. Pray with absolute trust in God's loving care for you. Let Him use you without consulting you. Let Jesus fill you with joy that you may preach without preaching."(*Love, a Fruit Always in Season* [San Francisco: Ignatius Pr., 1987], p. 26.)

May I share with you the excitement, the pure joy, the anticipation, the conviction and commitment I feel as I contemplate the great love our Heavenly Father has for each of us. As Nephi said, "When I desire to rejoice, my heart groaneth because of my sins; nevertheless, I know in whom I have trusted. My God hath been my support. . . . He hath filled me with his love, even unto the consuming of my flesh. . . . Behold, he hath heard my cry by day, and he hath given me knowledge by visions in the nighttime. . . .

"O then, if I have seen so great things, if the Lord in his condescension unto the children of men hath visited men in so much mercy, why should my heart weep and my soul linger in the valley of sorrow, and my flesh waste away, and my strength slacken, because of mine afflictions?

And why should I yield to sin, because of my flesh? Yea, why should I give way to temptations, that the evil one have place in my heart to destroy my peace and afflict my soul? Why am I angry because of mine enemy?

"Awake, my soul! No longer droop in sin. Rejoice, O my heart, and give place no more for the enemy of my soul." (2 Nephi 4:19, 21, 23, 26–28.)

And when we feel ourselves out of control, out of harmony, for a time, not knowing for certain where we are or where we are going spiritually, disappointed in our actions in relation to our desires, we need not despair. There is a place of spiritual repair. We can take our wounded spirits faithfully and regularly to the sacrament table and there renew our covenants, our commitments, by offering a broken heart and a contrite spirit. Then we begin, in part at least, to feel the healing and the peace that comes when we ponder the meaning of the atonement in our personal lives. May we each endure to the end and rejoice in the blessings of mortality through our consciousness of victory over self and communion with the infinite.

Chapter 7

Drifting, Dreaming, Directing

Of our day, Elder Bruce R. McConkie said, "Great trials lie ahead. All of the sorrows and perils of the past are but a foretaste of what is yet to be. And we must prepare ourselves temporally and spiritually." (*Ensign,* May 1979, p. 92.) Even with the reality of that kind of a backdrop, President Spencer W. Kimball admonished us, "Make no small plans, for they hold no magic to stir men's souls." (Regional Representatives seminar, 1979.) This reminds me of Dickens's *A Tale of Two Cities.* The story begins with the contrasts of that day:

"It was the best of times, it was the worst of times; it was the age of wisdom, it was the age of foolishness; it was the epic of belief, it was the epic of incredulity; it was the season of light, it was the season of darkness; it was the spring of hope, it was the winter of despair; we had everything before us, we had nothing before us; we were all going direct to heaven, we were all going direct the other way—in short—the period was so far like the present period, that some of its noisiest authorities insisted on it being received for good or for evil in a superlative degree of comparison only. . . . It was the year of our Lord one thousand seven hundred and seventy-five."

We are living in the times spoken of in the scriptures when peace shall be taken from the earth. Of our time President Kimball said, "To be a righteous woman is a glorious thing in any age. To be a righteous woman during the winding-up scenes on this earth, before the second coming of our Savior, is an especially noble calling. The righteous woman's strength and influence today can be tenfold what it might be in more tranquil times." (*My Beloved Sisters* [Deseret Book, 1979], p. 17.)

Each of us will determine whether this day spoken of as the great and dreadful day will be recorded in our journals of life as a truly great and glorious day in which we are privileged to take part, or if, in fact, it is recorded only as a day of turmoil, conflict, and confusion.

President Harold B. Lee was referring to our day, I believe, when he said: "We have some tight places to go before the Lord is through with this church and the world in this dispensation, which is the last dispensation, which shall usher in the coming of the Lord. The gospel was restored to prepare a people ready to receive him. There will be inroads within the Church. There will be, as President [N. Eldon] Tanner has said, 'Hypocrites—those professing, but secretly are full of dead men's bones.' We will see those who profess membership, but secretly are plotting and trying to lead people not to follow the leadership that the Lord has set up to preside in this church."

And knowing the nature of man, President Lee continued: "You may not like what comes from the authority of the Church. It may contradict your political views. It may contradict your social views. It may interfere with some of your social life. But if you listen to these things, as if from the mouth of the Lord himself, with patience and faith, the promise is that 'the gates of hell shall not prevail against you; yea, and the Lord God will disperse the powers of darkness from before you, and cause the heavens to shake for your good and his name's glory' (D&C 21:6)." (*Improvement Era*, December 1970, p. 126.)

It is while a person stands undecided, uncommitted, and uncovenanted, with choices waiting to be made, that vulnerability to every wind that blows becomes life-threatening. Uncertainty, the thief of time and commitment, breeds vacillation and confusion. It is in taking a stand and making a choice to follow our leaders that we become free to move forward. We are then released from the crippling position of doubtful indecision and confusion. We then have access to power and influence, so much so that we can hardly keep pace with our opportunities. It is in or by using our agency and making firm decisions that we turn the key.

Let me share with you a few lines from *The Agony and the Ecstasy* by Irving Stone. On the very brink of creating what for many has become his greatest masterpiece, Michelangelo is faced with a decision that, once made, must be lived with. He has completed a multitude of drawings suggesting hundreds of ways he might carve the David. He has been vacillating, contemplating, considering all the alternatives, the many options, weighing and waiting. Now he must make a choice:

> He burned his earlier drawings, settled down to the simplest beginning, probing within himself. . . . What could he find in David triumphant, he asked himself, worthy of sculpturing. Tradition portrayed him after the fact. Yet David after the battle was certainly an anticlimax, his great moment already gone. Which, then, was the important David? When did David become a giant? After killing Goliath, or at the moment he decided that he must try? David, as he was releasing with brilliant and deadly accuracy the shot from the sling; or David before he entered the battle when he decided that the Israelites must be freed from their vassalage to the Philistines? Was not the decision more important than the act itself, since character was more critical than action? For him, then, it was David's decision that made him a giant, not his killing of Goliath. This was the David he had been seeking, caught at the exultant height of resolution. . . . The man who killed Goliath would be committed all his life to warfare and its consequence: power. . . . To act was to join. David would not be sure he wanted to join. He had been a man alone. Once he tackled Goliath,

there would be no turning back. . . . It was what he sensed that he would do to himself, as well as what the world would do to him, that made him doubtful and averse in changing the pattern of his days. His had been a hard choice indeed. ([New York: Doubleday and Company, 1961], pp. 388, 390–91.)

It was in realizing the importance of David's hard choice and his faith to act that the door for Michelangelo was unlocked, allowing him to decide about his own mission in marble. Recognizing David as the giant at the moment of his decision allowed him to make his decision; and the choice having been made, his tempo changed and with it came strength, power, and hidden energies. Irving Stone's story continues:

> He soared, he drew with authority and power, he molded in clay . . . his fingers unable to keep pace with his thoughts and emotions, and with astonishing facility he knew where the David lay. The limitations of the block began to appear as assets, forcing his mind into a simplicity of design that might never have occurred to him had it been whole and perfect. The marble came alive now. (Ibid., p. 391.)

Each person must release his or her own David from the imperfect marble that holds it captive, and each of us will greatly hasten that process as we follow the counsel of the prophet. President Kimball said, "Be wise in the choices that you make. . . . Sharpen the skills you have been given and use the talents with which God has blessed you." (*Ensign,* November 1979, p. 103.) As we make right choices we are driven by an exhilaration that causes us to hunger and thirst and feel new energies that lift us, like Michelangelo, toward our goal.

As we make right choices, decisions, and commitments, we are released to move forward at a hastened pace and lengthen our stride. If we remain motionless on the brink of indecision we allow our voice, our example, our potential for good to be held imprisoned, as it were, in a slab of marble. Our testimonies, our commitments, and our covenants may lie deep inside, but until we can cut away all the debris that obscures this treasure, it cannot be recognized by others or even trusted by ourselves. As we seek divine direction, we will find our own blocks of marble to be more magnificent, with greater potential, than we have yet realized. Then, when the history of this era is reviewed, it might be said of us, as it was of Queen Esther, "Who knoweth whether thou art come to the kingdom for such a time as this?" (Esther 4:14.)

Even with these truths and inspiring examples before us, I feel concern for some who may feel discouraged, who may feel that we get our moralities mixed up with our realities and that the gulf between morality and reality is too big, the stakes are too high, the requirements too rigid, and the rewards too uncertain.

It has been my observation, and it is my confession as a former participant, that many people drift along with the crowd in the Church. Many good people drift to sacrament meeting and Sunday School, even family home evening, and they drift through a casual study of the scriptures. The drifters fall into at least one of two groups. In the first group are those who step into the mainstream, getting deeply involved with Church activity and floating with the current, comfortable with a sense of false security that they are in the right place. In the second group are those who, accepting a few selected principles, resist being part of the flow, the mainstream, and choose to get out into the eddies at the edge, freed from the demands of full participation. It is difficult to decide which of these two groups is better—or worse. Those of us who, on the basis of activity alone, are very much in the Church may not necessarily have the Church very much in us; and if we were to leave, the Church might hardly recognize the difference. Following the practices, doing the right thing but without coming to know, understand, accept, and apply the saving principles and doctrines, we may be compared to one who spends his entire life stringing the instrument but who never once hears the music for which the instrument was created, or who would be incapable of recognizing the music if he did listen.

In matters of principle, let us stand as solid as a rock. In matters of practice, may all that we do be based upon these saving principles, and may we understand the intrinsic relationship of principles and practices. In deciding to follow the admonition of our prophets to study the scriptures, we will gradually learn the doctrines that prepare us to stand on the rock of revelation and to experience less frequently the restless sense of drifting, wandering, questioning, and searching.

Many good people are very faithful in following the traditions and practices. I am reminded of a song we used to sing in Sunday School: "Never be late for the Sunday School class, / Come with your bright smiling faces." The chorus ended with this refrain: "Try to be there, always be there, / Promptly at ten in the morning." Starting Sunday School at ten in the morning was a practice, a tradition, for a long time. It was not a principle. Yet there were those among the faithful who felt uncomfortable about change, not unlike the feelings expressed by some today as practices and traditions are modified. When changes come, and they always will, for some it may be a test to survive because their foundation is based on practices alone, without an understanding of the eternal, unchanging principles.

Being faithful does not necessarily develop faith. The first principle of the gospel is faith in the Lord, Jesus Christ. To have faith in Him is to know Him, to know His doctrine, and to know that the course of our life is in harmony with and acceptable to Him. It is relatively easy to be faithful, but faith is born out of study, fasting, prayer, meditation, sacrifice, service, and, finally, personal revelation.

Glimpses of understanding come line upon line, precept

upon precept. Our Father is anxious to feed us just as fast
as we can handle it, but we regulate the richness and the
volume of our spiritual diet. And we do this by the same
method used by the sons of Mosiah: "They had waxed
strong in the knowledge of the truth; . . . they had searched
the scriptures diligently, that they might know the word of
God. But this is not all; they had given themselves to much
prayer, and fasting; therefore they had the spirit of
prophecy, and the spirit of revelation, and when they
taught, they taught with power and authority of God."
(Alma 17:2–3.)

Faithfulness without faith, practices without principles,
will leave us and our families seriously wanting as we
move closer to that time spoken of by Heber C. Kimball,
who said, "The time is coming when no man or woman will
be able to endure on borrowed light. Each will have to be
guided by the light within himself. If ye do not have it, you
will not stand." (Quoted by Harold B. Lee in *Conference
Report*, October 1955, p. 56.)

May we find ourselves doing less and less drifting as
we make right choices based on personal revelation that
give direction to us and our families each day of our life.
And with that direction, let us develop "a program for personal improvement" that will cause us to "reach for new
levels of achievement." (Spencer W. Kimball, *My Beloved
Sisters*, p. 20.) Certain principles are essential in our struggle
to avoid the wasteful experience of drifting.

Now, what of dreamers? Many of us are dreamers at
times, wanting in some way to escape ourselves, to be free
of our own limitations. I often ponder the words: "With vol-
untary dreams they cheat their minds." It has been said that
if fate would destroy a man, it would first separate his
forces and drive him to think one way and act another. It
would rob him of the contentment that comes only from
unity within. Choices must be decisive so that dreams and
actions can be in harmony with each other. When we do
something different than we know we should, it is like

going into a final examination and giving the wrong answer, even though we know the right one.

Dreaming, however, can also serve a very positive function when it fits Webster's definition of having "a goal or purpose ardently desired."

In the popular musical *South Pacific* is the delightful song that asks, "If you don't have a dream, how ya gonna have a dream come true?" I am concerned for some of our sisters who have a magnificent dream but who will never fully realize its fulfillment because they feel that a righteous husband will take care of it, and they fail to prepare for their part in this eternal partnership.

There are some sisters who ponder the administrative structure of the Church and trouble themselves with what they think they don't have without ever coming to a full understanding of their own special and unique mission and the great blessings reserved specifically for them. We hear it expressed in terms that suggest that because women don't have the priesthood, they are shortchanged.

Still other sisters have the misunderstanding that priesthood is synonymous with men, and so they excuse themselves and have no concern for studying its importance in their own lives. The term *priesthood* is used without qualification, whether it refers to a bearer of the priesthood, to priesthood blessings, or to priesthood ordinances. Regardless of how it is used, our hearts should cry and we should raise our voices and shout warnings to sisters whose dreams are built on such faulty foundations.

Our greatest dreams will be fulfilled only as we come to understand fully and experience the blessings of the priesthood, the power of the priesthood, and the ordinances of the priesthood in our own lives. If we were to begin with the time a child is given a name and a blessing and then continue on through baptism, confirmation, the sacrament, callings and being set apart, patriarchal blessings, administrations, the endowment, and finally celestial marriage, we would quickly realize that all the saving blessings of the priesthood are for everyone, male and female.

And while the divine mission of motherhood is paramount, it is not all-inclusive. To help another gain eternal life is a companion privilege. This privilege, indeed this sacred responsibility, this noblest of callings, is denied to no worthy person. To assist in bringing to pass the eternal life of man, and to do it in dignity and honor, is the very pinnacle of my own personal dream. And for us to close our eyes to these eternal truths and not recognize them as priesthood blessings and ordinances is to keep us on the fringe area of the very saving principles that can make our eternal dreams come true.

It is true that as sisters we do not experience a priesthood ordination that carries an administrative function. We also do not have the tremendous, weighty burden of having that sacred responsibility heaped upon us in addition to the mission of creating and nurturing in partnership with God, first in giving birth to the Lord's spirit children and then in raising those children to serve the Lord and keep his commandments. I have come to know that we can all, both men and women, rejoice in the sacred calling of motherhood. To give birth is but one part of this sacred calling.

After drifting and dreaming, now may we consider the directing of one's life. At my high school graduation, Elder Oscar A. Kirkham of the First Council of the Seventy stood at the pulpit, looking into the eyes of idealistic, enthusiastic graduates, and offered this challenge: "Build a seaworthy ship. Be a loyal shipmate, and sail a true course." I don't remember anything else that he said, or what anyone else said, for that matter. But I've pondered that challenge many times over the years. In directing our lives, we want to be sure of the true course and its ultimate destination. We cannot risk being caught in the disillusionment of the fellow who was committed to going north and was in fact traveling north—but on an iceberg that was floating south.

True points, like stars in the heavens to guide us, are readily available for anyone earnestly seeking direction. These true points of doctrine are found in the true church. (See D&C 11:16.) Conversion to the truth comes by accepting true doctrine, and the truth of doctrine can be known only by revelation gained as a result of obedience. The Savior taught: "My doctrine is not mine, but his that sent me. If any man will do his will, he shall know of the doctrine, whether it be of God, or whether I speak of myself." (John 7:16–17.)

The skeptic of two thousand years ago might have said, "Look, if I knew for sure that the star (the sign of the Savior's birth) would appear in the heavens tonight, I would be obedient." That's like standing in front of a stove and saying, "Give me some heat, and then I'll put in the wood." We must put in the wood first, and then we feel the warmth and the heat; then we can bear testimony of its reality. In the twelfth chapter of Ether we read: "Dispute not because ye see not, for ye receive no witness until after the trial of your faith." (Ether 12:6.) As our faith is tried and we are found standing firm even in times of storm, we will rejoice with increased confidence and discover within ourselves the loyal shipmate that we really have as we sail a true course.

Apostles and prophets have been provided in the Church for the purposes of identifying and teaching true doctrine, lest men be "tossed to and fro, and carried about with every wind of doctrine." (Ephesians 4:14.) Now, we can follow the Brethren blindly, as one of my non-Mormon friends claims that we do—and I might add that it is far safer and better to follow them blindly than not at all—but that could be an abdication of our responsibility to direct our own lives and become spiritually independent. Following the practices alone is not enough. We must come to know the reason, indeed the doctrinal basis, for that practice; otherwise, when the practice or tradition is questioned or changed, those who do not understand the principle are prone to waver. They may even abandon or reject the very practice intended as a schoolmaster to carry them to an understanding of a saving and eternal principle.

There were those in King Benjamin's time who were caught up in following the law of Moses. With blinders they followed the practices—an eye for an eye and a tooth for a tooth—until King Benjamin taught them that their practices availed them nothing unless they accepted the mission of the Savior and His atonement. Without that commitment their practices were for naught.

While Adam was offering the firstlings of the flock, an angel appeared and asked him why he was doing it. Adam responded, "I know not, save the Lord commanded me." The practice was offering sacrifice, but the principle, in this instance, was obedience. And then Adam received a witness, after the trial of his faith. The angel explained: "This thing is a similitude of the sacrifice of the Only Begotten of the Father." (Moses 5:6–7.)

As we direct our lives, it is important to understand practices and principles, their relationship as well as the differences between them. In my mind's eye, I visualize the practices as a horizontal line, a foundation, a schooling, a testing, a preparation; and I see the saving and exalting eternal principles or doctrine as a vertical line that links our souls to heaven and builds the relationship with God and faith in the Lord, Jesus Christ, and His mission.

There continues to be much opposition to true doctrine; but by and by the storm subsides, the clouds disperse, the sun breaks forth, and the rock of truth is seen again, firm and lasting. There never was a true principle that was not met by storm after storm of opposition and abuse, until that principle had obtained such influence that it no longer paid to oppose it. But until that time, the opposition and the abuse have ebbed and flowed like the tide.

It was a strong doctrine that rid Jesus of his weak disciples, and the same testing process continues today in determining those worthy of His kingdom. The Prophet

Joseph Smith stated: "God has in reserve a time . . . when He will bring all His subjects, who have obeyed His voice and kept His commandments, into His celestial rest. This rest is of such perfection and glory, that man has need of a preparation before he can, according to the laws of that kingdom, enter it and enjoy its blessings. This being the fact, God has given certain laws to the human family, which, if observed, are sufficient to prepare them to inherit this rest. This, then, we conclude was the purpose of God in giving his laws to us." (*Teachings of the Prophet Joseph Smith,* 1976, p. 54.)

In our goal to apply principles and proceed with direction, it isn't intended that we arrive before we experience that witness of the Spirit. The witness sustains us in our journey. Truman Madsen has observed: "The greatest tragedy of life is that having paid that awful price of suffering 'according to the flesh that his bowels might be filled with compassion' and now prepared to reach down and help us, [the Savior] is forbidden because we won't let him. We look down instead of up." ("Prayer and the Prophet Joseph," *Ensign,* January 1976, p. 23.) We choose to remain enclosed in marble. But if we would free ourselves and come to know this truth through personal revelation, the time might come when even our routine practices could become life-giving and done in the Lord's name with His spirit so that the whole of our lives becomes a sacred experience as we labor for Him continuously.

Not long ago I witnessed what until then had been something of a routine for me, the blessing on the food. Picture with me my aged father, his body deteriorated by the devastation of stomach cancer, but his spirit magnified and refined through suffering. He sat at the kitchen table; he then weighed less than a hundred pounds. Bowing his head, resting it in his frail, trembling hands over a spoonful of baby food—all that he could eat—he pronounced a blessing on the food, as though it were a sacred sacrament, and gave thanks with acceptance and submission, with truth and faith, because he knew to whom he was speaking.

It is in coming to know our Savior and the saving principles taught through the gospel of Jesus Christ that we become different. And we need to be recognized as being different. The majority of the world doesn't see the options. It is our responsibility to be obviously good and obviously right—and able to articulate our values and be advocates for truth. We may have a temple recommend and attend our meetings and practice the principles, but how we look and act, what we say and do, may be the only message some people will receive. Our acts should show that there is a power and an influence with us that the inhabitants of the world do not understand. What is it that distinguishes us from others? The distinction is that we profess to be guided by revelation. And it is because of this principle that we are peculiar, since all of our actions can be under divine guidance. Having made the choice, we must stand and be visibly different. Until we make that choice, we remain anonymous, subject to the current of meandering multitudes.

President Kimball said: "Much of the major growth that is coming to the Church in the last days will come because many of the good women of the world (in whom there is often such an inner sense of spirituality) will be drawn to the Church in large numbers. This will happen to the degree that the women of the Church reflect righteousness and articulateness in their lives and to the degree that they are seen as distinct and different—in happy ways—from the women of the world." (*My Beloved Sisters*, p. 44.)

That is our direction. That is our challenge.

All individuals are what they are and where they are by a composite of choices that direct their lives each day. The responsibility of directing is not only for our own lives, but also for others who may be looking for the light. As we build a seaworthy ship and then sail a true course, many sails will navigate safely through troubled waters into the peaceful harbor because of the unflickering light radiating from the bow of our craft. As I consider our responsibility to others, I am inspired by the words of one of our hymns:

> *Brightly beams our Father's mercy*
> *From his lighthouse evermore,*
> *But to us he gives the keeping*
> *Of the lights along the shore.*
> —*Hymns, no. 335*

Elder Neal A. Maxwell has written, "As other lights flicker and fade, the light of the gospel will burn ever more brightly in a darkening world, guiding the humble but irritating the guilty and those who prefer the dusk of decadence." (*Church News*, January 5, 1970, p. 28.)

May our lights be bright, without a flicker, as we tend the lights along the shore. Let us reach out and touch one another. Let us help carry one another's burdens. In cooperation we can overcome great odds. Let us rejoice with one another. It may be just a smile, a note, a call, an encouraging word that says, "I care. I understand. I will stand by you and help you." These are life-saving measures in times of storm.

Recently I was privileged to read part of a blessing received by one of our sisters that stated that her life would continue over a period when she would see great devastation and that she would be called to go into homes of the sorrowing, the suffering, the sick and afflicted, to minister unto them, to bind up their wounds, and to cheer them. I believe that we have all been called to minister unto those in need, to bind up not just their physical wounds but also their spiritual wounds, social wounds, and wounds that are kept hidden, sometimes festering until someone cares enough to tend the lights along the shore.

These are matters of eternal consequence, and we can,

if we desire, reach far enough to experience an awakening of things we have known before.

It is my fervent and humble testimony that the heavens are very much open to women today. They are not closed unless we ourselves, by our choices, close them. And this reality can be just as evident as in any time past. As I read of the great spirituality of women of the past and realize how the Lord communicated with them, I thrill with the spiritual manifestations that accompanied their missions in life, literally a power evidencing the will of God made known through their instrumentality. I think of Eliza R. Snow, of whom Joseph F. Smith said, "She walked not in the borrowed light of others, but faced the morning unafraid and invincible."

The Spirit whispers to me that there are Eliza R. Snows among us even today, and there can be many, many more. We can pull down the blessings of heaven through obedience to law. These divine and sacred blessings are not reserved for others alone. Visions and revelations come by the power of the Holy Ghost. The Lord has said, "On my servants and on my handmaidens I will pour out in those days of my Spirit; and they shall prophesy." (Acts 2:18.)

Let us go forth with the faith, the vision, the direction, and the decision to abide the laws that ensure these blessings not only for ourselves and our families but for all of God's children everywhere. Let us each feel deeply the power and strength and influence for good of our collective and united resolves. With renewed determination and confidence and commitment to the covenants we have made, let us become truly and in every way "women of God." Let us go forth in faith and confidence and prepare for the noble calling spoken of by the Prophet—to be righteous women during the winding-up scenes on this earth before the second coming of our Savior.

Chapter 8

The Joy of the Journey

Early one morning, as a child, I walked beside my father along the irrigation ditch at the lower level of our eighty acres in Alberta, Canada. Then, standing at the edge of the ditch with his shovel in his hand, Dad said, "I'm going to teach you to jump the ditch." And he added, as he often did when teaching me something, " . . . if your attitude is right." I watched him place the shovel in the middle of the ditch and hop over; then he hopped back again the same way. He anchored the shovel in the ditch and pushed the handle toward me.

I looked down at the ditch, which seemed to be getting wider and wider, as the water got deeper and deeper. "But, Dad," I asked, "what if I don't make it?" He smiled and explained, "You'll land in the water and get soaked." "Then what?" I asked. "You'll still need to get to the other side." As I stared at the water skitters on the surface of the water, he provided more encouragement. "See that clump of buffalo beans on the other side? Keep your eye on those buffalo beans and give it all you've got, and you'll make it." Taking a deep breath, I held tight to the handle of the shovel and gave it all I had. I landed right on top of the buffalo beans. Quickly I looked back and saw Dad with both hands clasped in the air and a big smile. "I knew you could do it," he said. Then he jumped across with great ease. I wondered why all the fuss just for me.

Later in the day, eating our lunch in the shade of the elm trees, Dad and I talked about my experience in jumping the ditch. He looked more serious than before as he taught me this greatest of all lessons. "Ardie," he said, "there are many ditches you will have to cross in life and many of them you'll have to cross alone. If you keep your eye on the other side and give it all you've got, you'll make it."

Sometimes we lose sight of our goals because we become distracted by things that for a time seem more important. President Kimball gave us valuable counsel when he said, "Since immortality and eternal life constitute the sole purpose of life, all other interests and activities are but incidental thereto."

You might say, "You mean dinner parties, travel, nice homes, and entertainment are not important?" To some people they may be important, but they are not essential. We don't have to know everything; we don't have to do everything; we don't have to have everything. We just have to know who we really are, and what we should do, and why we should do it—the very purpose of life.

The answer to each of these important questions is clearly explained in the gospel of Jesus Christ. In fact, the gospel is the plan of salvation, intended for all of our Father's children so that none may be denied. The first great principle is that God is our Eternal Father and we are His children. In our premortal life we accepted His plan, which is the only plan through which we can gain eternal life, His greatest gift to us His children.

The first Young Women Value states, "I am a daughter of a Heavenly Father who loves me, and I will have faith in His eternal plan which centers in Jesus Christ, my Savior." Jesus, our Elder Brother, invites us to follow Him, and He has provided the way for us to do so. He has given us commandments that we must obey if we would return to our heavenly home. But He does not force us; He has also given us our agency. It is an eternal truth that progression requires the right to make our own choices. We must be free to choose for ourselves and then be accountable for our choices and accept the consequences.

Commandments are brief statements of direction given by God that are consistent with eternal laws and that provide eternal blessings. In a similar way, during our sojourn on earth, earthly parents establish family rules or commandments to help provide protection for their children while they learn to make wise choices.

How well I remember fighting the restrictions early in my life. One evening I attended a Sunday School party at the home of one of my friends. My parents had told me I was to be home by 10:00, which I remember thinking was quite unreasonable for my "mature" age. At about 10:15, I said to myself, "If a knock comes on the door right now, I'll just die. It will probably be my father." Right then came the knock. It was my father. Humiliated in front of my friends, I wanted to die. As we walked along the gravel road to our home, I thought, "Dad, how could you embarrass me like this in front of my friends?" It was a most memorable and painful experience.

A few years later, I went with a group of friends to a dance in Cardston at Christmastime. The weather was extremely cold, forty degrees below zero, with a strong wind blowing the snow around. At the end of the dance we headed toward the turnoff that would take us home. We were about halfway there when the car slowed to a gradual putt-putt and stopped. Thick frost quickly coated the car windows when the engine was turned off. In that extreme cold, we knew our lives were in danger. We had heard of people who had abandoned their cars in a blizzard and had gotten lost and died. We had also heard of others who had remained in their cars and had frozen to death.

After two or three moments of silence and private prayer, one of the youths in the back seat asked, "How long do you think it will be before your dad will get here?" What made them think my dad would come after us? Because he always did. Looking at our watches, we estimated the earliest possible time he might arrive. We scraped the heavy frost with our fingernails to make a little window so we could see out. At the shortest possible time, one of my friends put his eye to the small opening and excitedly cried, "He's coming. He's coming!" Suddenly we could see a glimmer of light through the blizzard, and it seemed to be getting brighter and brighter. My father had arrived. He had come to our rescue, to take us home.

One time I wanted to die because my dad came after me; another time my friends and I lived because he came after us.

Today there is a storm raging. It is no ordinary storm, not the kind with a temperature of forty degrees below zero. But make no mistake, lives are in danger. President Ezra Taft Benson reminds us, "Never before on the face of the earth have the forces of evil and the forces of good been so well organized. While our generation will be comparable in wickedness to the days of Noah when the Lord cleansed the earth by a flood, there is a major difference this time. God has saved for the final inning some of His stronger and most valiant children who will help bear off the kingdom triumphantly. You are the generation that must be prepared to meet your God. The final outcome is certain. The forces of righteousness will finally win; but what remains to be seen is where each of us personally, now and in the future, will stand in this battle and how tall we will stand."

Some people are giving in or giving up because they lack the vision, the faith, and the hope to survive and overcome. But with an understanding of the gospel of Jesus Christ, we have not only the vision but also the promises and the blessings and the help. The help comes from our Savior, Jesus Christ. Sin is a conscious violation of a true principle. How Jesus saw sin as wrong! But He saw it springing from deep and unmet needs on the part of the sinner. He paid the price for us. He atoned for our sins. He is our Savior. And we partake of that great sacrifice, that blessing, as we choose to live in harmony with eternal laws and accept the saving ordinances and covenants. The covenants we make with our Father in heaven secure our safe journey, even a joyful journey. They allow us to keep our eye on the buffalo beans, so to speak, and give it all we've got, knowing that when we do, we will succeed.

I am impressed with the story told of Florence Chadwick, who, at thirty-four years of age, determined to be the first woman to swim the twenty-two miles from Catalina Island to the California coast. She had already been the first woman to swim the English Channel in both directions. One writer reported the experience:

"The water was cold that July morning, and the fog was so thick she could hardly see the boats in her own party. Millions were watching on national television. Several times sharks, which had gotten too close, had to be driven away with rifles to protect the lone figure in the water. As the hours ticked off, she swam on. Fatigue had never been her big problem in these swims. It was the bone-chilling cold of the water. More than fifteen hours later, numbed with cold, she asked to be taken out. She couldn't go on. Her mother and her trainer alongside in a boat told her they were near land. They urged her not to quit. But when she looked toward the California coast, all she could see was the dense fog."

A few minutes later, at 15 hours and 55 minutes, she was taken out of the water. It was not until hours later, when her body began to warm up again, that she felt the shock of failure. To a reporter she blurted out, "Look, I'm not excusing myself, but if I could have just seen land I might have made it." She had been pulled out only one-half mile from the California coast. Later she reflected that she had been defeated not by fatigue, not even the cold, but by fog. It had defeated her because it had obscured her goal and blinded her reason, her eyes, her heart. This was the only time Florence Chadwick ever quit. Two months later she swam that same channel and again fog obscured her view, but this time she swam with her faith intact. Somewhere behind that fog was land.

Yes, there are a lot of sharks and a lot of fog and fatigue and chilling cold. It is all part of the test. We don't have to do great things. We just have to hang on and do right things that become great. And while life may not always be enjoyable, it can be very satisfying and rewarding.

Let me refer again to the Young Women Values, which are really gospel principles for all of us, a basis for decision-making, helping us keep our eye on the goal. The values of faith, divine nature, and individual worth help us understand our identity and our relationship to our Father and His Son, Jesus Christ. Then we focus on the importance of knowledge. We must have knowledge to make wise choices.

Samuel the Lamanite said in the Book of Mormon, "And now remember, remember, . . . that whosoever perisheth, perisheth unto himself; and whosoever doeth iniquity, doeth it unto himself; for behold, ye are free; ye are permitted to act for yourselves; for behold, God hath given unto you a knowledge and he hath made you free. He hath given unto you that ye might know good from evil, and he hath given unto you that ye might choose life or death." (Helaman 14:30–31.)

Considering the importance of gaining knowledge, remember that if we want to experience the sense of smell, we use our nose, not our ears or eyes. If we want to hear, we use our ears, not our nose. If we want to see, we use our eyes, not our ears. And if we want to experience spiritual things, we must develop spiritual receptivity. We must not remain in grade one in spiritual things while we charge ahead in secular knowledge. As Elder Jeffrey R. Holland has said, "Be prepared so that if you are an engineer and want to cross the Red Sea, you will be prepared to construct a bridge or part the water."

I am reminded of the story of a visitor to the famous art museum, the Louvre, in Paris. When told of the value of one of the masterpieces there, he scoffed. "I can't see why it should be priced so high," he said. And the curator simply responded, "But don't you wish you could?"

Secular and spiritual knowledge prepares us to make wise choices and add to the joy of the journey. There may be times when we feel discouraged and painfully aware of our limited capacity to grasp it all, with so much to learn and so little time. But we don't need to grasp it all, not all at once, and not all here during this part of our journey. However, we want to learn as much as possible, because we are promised that "whatever principle of intelligence we attain unto in this life, it will rise with us in the resurrection. And if a person gains more knowledge and intelligence in this life through his diligence and obedience than another, he will have so much the advantage in the world to come." (D&C 130:18–19.)

I recall vividly as a child the painful experience of feeling "dumb" and struggling through the darkness of discouragement when you feel everyone else is smart. I believed that being smart was the greatest blessing one could ever have, and that gave me concern for what God would think of someone who was dumb.

I have found that usually our greatest lessons come in times of anguish, perhaps because we are more teachable. My anxiety was quieted somewhat on one occasion when my parents walked around the Cardston Temple and explained that if I continued to do my very best in school, I should no longer worry about being dumb, but should focus on being good. If I was good enough and obedient in keeping God's commandments, they said, one day instead of walking around the outside of the temple, I could go inside. And there—and only there—I would learn all I needed to know to return to my Heavenly Father. They explained that all the knowledge in the world would be of little consequence if I failed to gain the gift of knowledge that would be available to me in the temple. And they reassured me that I was smart enough to learn all I really needed to know to accomplish my earthly mission. This was a great comfort to me at that difficult time.

Only in The Church of Jesus Christ of Latter-day Saints, guided by a living prophet receiving continuous revelation, and only by living worthy to enter the temple, can we receive the temple endowment, the gift of knowledge. There we receive sacred ordinances and make covenants that guide us through our life and provide the very purpose for this earth life and preparation for the next.

May God bless us to focus on eternal life while enjoying the valleys and mountain peaks along the journey.

Chapter 9

There Is Time Enough

Every year I find myself becoming more and more concerned about health, perhaps because a friend warns me
that after forty years of age, it's patch, patch, patch. Thus,
preserving, maintaining, and restoring emotional and physical health has become a high priority for me, as I am sure
it is for you. I heard the other day of a lady much older than
I who had completed fifty pushups that very morning. That
was distressing to me until I learned that she had begun
them a year ago! It's fun to be able to laugh at some of the
things we can't control, but it is equally important for us to
feel that we can manage the things over which we can have
control.

Dr. Verla Collins, an associate with Intermountain
Hospital Corporation, once told me that there is evidence
to verify that approximately 87 percent of the illnesses that
are medically treated can be linked to psychosomatic illnesses. William James, often referred to as the father of psy-
chology, stated, "Neither the nature nor the amount of our
work is accountable for the frequency and severity of our
breakdown, but the cause rather lies in the observed feelings of hurry and having no time. Breathlessness, tension,
anxiety, the lack of inner harmony and ease." Louis Pasteur
said it this way: "The microbe is nothing, but it is the ter-
rain." In other words, the condition or state of the body is

what matters most. A body under stress, in the state of "dis-ease," is more vulnerable to disease.

And so we might ask, Do I have time enough to allow me to move through life in a state of ease rather than dis-ease? Time is used in different ways by different people. Historians record time, referees call time, musicians mark time, prisoners serve time, loafers kill time, and most of us try to stretch time as though we had an unlimited bank account. Often we find ourselves overdrawn.

In the bank of life, there are just so many hours in every day. We cannot overdeposit, but we can overdraw. Bankruptcy puts us in a state of tension. In life we use time, kill it, spend it, call it, save it, and wonder where it goes. It seems as though we never have enough time, and yet we have all there is. Time clicks off one second at a time, and we set a rhythm as it goes. Is there enough? Are we ever guilty of building prison walls that tie us up with tension and with anxiety when we utter just five little words, "I do not have time"? And yet we tell ourselves we don't have enough time—when we have all that there is.

There is always time enough if we will apply it well. We do this by first learning how to separate the vital things in life, which are really very few, from the urgent things, which are constantly mounting. When we learn that "urgent" is not the same thing as "vital," we begin to take control of our lives instead of having life control us. Too often, we respond as though everything were vital instead of just urgent.

Let me give you an example. Remember when you were in school and you started the semester with three papers to write and four textbooks to read? Were those assignments vital or urgent? They were vital to the graduation, but were they urgent? When did they become urgent? Often not until the night before they were due. What robbed you of the time when you could be taking care of the vital? All the urgent things—the social obligations, the sale downtown, the call on the phone, and so on. Many times we don't separate the vital from the urgent.

Some things really are urgent, but the vital tasks rarely need to be done immediately. The urgent ones grab for our attention, our energy, and often our commitment. We live by the belief that we should get something done now, and when all the little things are cleared out of the way, we can get to the big things. Often, however, the things that initially seemed vital are forgotten, and with a sense of loss we realize we have become slaves to the urgent, the social pressures, the demands, or the expectations that *we* thought that *they* thought we ought to do.

Our time is our life. Whatever it is we are doing with our time, we are paying for it with our life. So what are we getting for our life today?

Too often I fear we are distracted from the few things in life that are really important because of a sense of urgency—too many things in too many places for too many people with too little time and too few rewards. Yet the scripture tells us, "Be still, and know that I am God." (Psalm 46:10.) We also read of Joshua, who must have felt great pressure to bring all of the people to the Jordan and get them across the river. Remember the counsel he was given? "When ye are come to the brink of the water of Jordan, ye shall stand still in Jordan." (Joshua 3:8.) Stand still. Take time to get your head on straight. Call on all the resources available before you start rushing ahead.

Years ago in California in a little wooded area, I read a pamphlet called "The Parable of the Redwood." In it was this statement: "If you stand very still in the heart of a wood, you will hear many wonderful things—the snap of a twig, the wind in the trees, and the whine of invisible things. If you stand very still in the turmoil of life, and you wait for the voice from within, you will draw from the silence the things that you need, strength, hope, faith, courage for your task."

A recent best-selling book, *Megatrends,* discusses the

mounting number of choices available today: more alternatives, more paths to take, more things to succeed. We talk
about a knowledge explosion, an information explosion.
Walk through any library and look at all the books you'll
never have a chance to read in this life. Think of all the
things you don't know and that you won't have a chance to
be accountable for. Because we have so many choices, this
is either the best of all times or the worst of all times.
Having so many alternatives can be a burden—what one
writer has called "the burden of over-choice"—or a blessing, depending on our ability to separate the vital from the
urgent or the trivial.

Ralph Waldo Emerson said, "There comes a time in
every man's education when he arrives at the conclusion
that envy is ignorance and imitation, suicide. But he must
take himself for better or for worse as his allotted portion.
And all the good earth be full of good. No kernel of nourishing corn can come to him but by the toil bestowed by
him upon that plot of ground given to him to till. The
power within him is new in nature. No one knows what it
is he can do, nor does he know until he has tried."

What each of us must do, then, is all that concerns us
individually, not what others may say. That rule, which is
as difficult to follow in actual as in intellectual life, is the
sole distinction between greatness and meanness. It is even
more difficult because there are always those who think
they know our duty better than we know it. It is easy in the
world to live after the opinions of the world, and in solitude
to live after our own. But the great person is the one who in
the midst of the crowd keeps with perfect sweetness the
independence of solitude.

In this hurry-hurry world, we must provide time for
solitude. Sometimes we call it meditation. Anne Morrow
Lindbergh, in her book *A Gift from the Sea,* talks about the
soul's quieting inside from the turmoil of the world. We
must find that peace, a moment in time to pull ourselves

away from the world so that we can pull ourselves together to face the world.

And so it is that we take ourselves away for just a while, for whatever reason, to focus on what we value most so that we can let go of the things that we don't value as much. It is in relation to what we really value that we form a foundation for how we live our lives—what we will and what we won't do. Planning is important in helping us to manage our time. It helps bring the future into the present so that we can begin to take control. For example, suppose we want to take a vacation next summer. We don't wait until summer comes to start planning and looking at a map. We begin now so that when the time comes and we leave on our vacation, we are in control.

Another advantage of planning is that it helps us live in a state of anticipation. Anytime we have a plan, we are in a mode of anticipation. We may get tired but we will never get bored, because planning helps us begin to be in control, to refuse to give up what we want most for what we want now. For example, right now I may want to sleep, or I may want a new car, or I may want freedom from schedules. But more than that, I want education, or I want to be with my family, or I want to serve my fellowman. I can't do it all.

So how do we make the most of our time? We do it by planning. Goal setting is a form of planning. We set a goal and then we plan how we are going to achieve it. But we also have to set priorities. We can't do everything; we have to let some things go so that we can make others a reality. And when that happens, we begin to have little signs of success. This increases our self-confidence, our self-esteem, our productivity; and as we climb up little by little, eventually we reach that valued goal.

Having goals without any values as their foundation can be likened to a willow that responds to every breeze that blows. Without goals or plans, we will never have time enough, and we will respond to every distraction that comes along—and nothing important will ever get done. But if our goals are anchored in values, we will have time enough, for we will set priorities to ensure that we reach our goals. We will be in control. That is when freedom comes. That is when the stress level begins to go down.

To illustrate, suppose you come home from a day of whatever you've been about, and your neighbor says, "I've picked and put up two bushels of apricots today and taken seven quarts over to one of my neighbors, and my house is clean, and I'm happy, and it's been a glorious day." Then you walk in your house and look out the window and see the apricots that are on the ground around your tree, and you think, "Oh, I don't even have my apricots picked!" If you don't have a plan, you'll pull the blinds and say to yourself, "I wish that neighbor would move away." The pressure is too great, and you feel threatened by what someone else is doing.

However, if you have a plan, a valued goal, you may say, "I spent this day with my widowed, elderly mother. And frankly, my family doesn't even like apricots." When we know why we are doing what we are doing, we don't need to worry about why another person is doing what she is doing. And that is a wonderful relief.

A basis for decision-making or planning has to be related to the things that we value most. Goals can change with times and seasons and circumstances. Perhaps you have been with a friend and you have thought, "Oh, I want to be as knowledgeable about literature as she is." So you resolve to take a literature class. Then you are with another friend and you think, "I want to be as good a cook as she is"—and you decide to enroll in gourmet cooking class. Why do we do this? We do it because we are blessed with so many opportunities. But blessing or burden depends on whether or not we decide what we value most, set our goals, and then begin to make a plan.

I like the words of Joan of Arc in the play *Joan of Lorraine* by Maxwell Anderson. Her words serve as a reminder to us.

She says, "I know this now, every man gives his life for what he believes. Every woman gives her life for what she believes. Sometimes people believe in little or nothing. Nevertheless they give their lives to that little or nothing. One life is all we have. We live it as we believe in living it, and then it's gone. But to surrender what you are and live without belief, that's more terrible than dying. More terrible than dying young."

What do we believe? What are we willing to live for? We sometimes talk about what we are willing to die for, but what are we willing to live for? If we say we really value something and we are not giving any time to it, we are in a state of tension. We are in a state of dis-ease. There is time enough when we establish our values and set our priorities. We can't have everything, but there is enough time for the things that matter most.

An important element in planning is to plan with a purpose. Instead of asking what we should do, we should ask ourselves what we want to have happen. This then becomes the basis for our plans and our decisions.

Recently someone said to my husband, who is partially retired, "You have a little time. I have a deal for you—an opportunity for you to make some really good money. The product is good, and you'll have a lot of flexibility. You can do it when you want to do it." So we sat down and talked about this great opportunity. We asked ourselves, "What would we do with the extra money? We eat all we want, we have all the clothes we need, our house is big enough, and we have enough to meet our needs." The "opportunity" sounded pretty good until we tested it against our highest values and our goals. The value of our time together was more important than the value of other things we could get with more money.

When we sit down for a family activity, typically we ask, "What shall we do?" A better question would be, "What do we want to have happen?" We shouldn't wait until we get this bill paid or that project completed before we begin to establish valued goals. There is time enough even now. If we wait until tomorrow to begin to plan, when tomorrow comes we will still be waiting for the future.

Yes, there is time enough if we set our priorities and plan with a purpose, with our values in place. May we each have time enough so that when we look back, the things that we wanted most were not sacrificed for the things of least importance.

Part III

Our Eternal Families

Chapter 10

With No Vision, the Family Perishes

On occasion when I participate in youth conferences, I will sometimes ask the young people if they have discovered that their parents aren't perfect. There is always an immediate response in the affirmative. I follow with a second question: "Are you aware that they don't have any perfect children either?" That usually comes as a surprise. The fact is, none of us is perfect. We are placed on earth in families according to an eternal plan that affords the most ideal structure for our growth and development.

One faithful and somewhat idealistic mother reportedly was determined to rid her family of all distracting influences in the home, beginning with negative comments. To put this plan into effect, she announced that the next person who spoke an unkind word would have his or her mouth washed out with soap. Now with any threat, there must be follow-up. In response to the question of whether or not she followed up, she admitted, "Yes, I did, and it tasted terrible."

And so it is with each of us in our family relationships. We know where we are. We are not yet perfect. We are in the process of perfection as we prepare for eternal life. An understanding of this ultimate goal helps keep individuals and families on course, on schedule, and moving forward according to the eternal plan.

Today a battle is being waged, and it is no ordinary

battle. The safety, the protection, the survival, the sanctity of the family are under attack as never before. The traditional family structure is disintegrating, and many individuals are suffering deep and serious wounds. There is an increasing number of casualties. Problems with crime, drugs, alcohol, immorality, abuse, and even suicide are growing at an alarming rate. This is no ordinary battle. The enemy is real, and the family is the target.

In the fight against the devastating influences that press upon even the most traditional and solid families, it is important to keep in mind the vision of where we ultimately want to be. An understanding of all that is past and the promises of the future helps give us the vision to make daily decisions of eternal consequence. Without discernment or foresight to see beyond the urgencies or apparent crises of the moment, one can win the battle but lose the war.

In His infinite mercy, God has revealed to us a great vision concerning the family. The knowledge that God is our Father and we are His children places the family unit in the most exalted position. Think of it: we existed with Him in a family relationship as His children! We were faithful, valiant, and obedient; and, despite the opposing forces there, we chose to keep our first estate and then to come to this mortal life knowing it would be a time of severe trials and testing.

We have been told that we will experience opposition in all things and learn to act for ourselves. (See 2 Nephi 2:16.) This mortal life provides the opportunities for us to qualify ourselves to become joint-heirs with Jesus Christ, to establish eternal family relationships through the sealing power of the priesthood, and to have eternal increase in the celestial kingdom.

With the vision of our next home, we can gain a better understanding of our existence here and the importance of our family relationships. The more aware we are that the spirit world is an extension of our mortal existence, the better prepared we are to set aside the treasures of this world and to establish priorities in relation to the next.

As we learn to live in such a way that the vision of eternity presses upon us, we will make decisions that may not be popular in society but will be in harmony with the Lord's plan. President Brigham Young once said that if he could do but one thing to bless the Saints, he believed it would be to give them "eyes with which to see things as they are." (*Journal of Discourses* 3:221.) We seek to know the truth, to gain "knowledge of things as they are, and as they were, and as they are to come." (D&C 93:24.)

President Kimball explained that "one of the ordinances performed in the temple is that of the endowment, which comprises a course of instruction relating to the eternal journey of a man and woman from the pre-earthly existence through the earthly experience and on to the exaltation each may attain." (*The Teachings of Spencer W. Kimball* [Bookcraft, 1982], p. 535.)

An understanding of this plan and faith in God will provide the strength for us to endure the most severe trials and struggles and to sacrifice everything necessary to reach the goal of eternal family relationships. It has been so in the past and continues to be so today.

Some time ago my husband and I visited the Mormon Cemetery at Winter Quarters, a monument to family members, young and old, who were buried in graves along the trail as their families continued westward toward the Rocky Mountains. Of those people, who had vision and faith in God, we read: "There are times and places in the life of every individual, every people, and every nation when great spiritual heights are reached, . . . when courage becomes a living thing, . . . when faith in God stands as the granite mountain wall, firm and immovable. . . . Winter Quarters . . . was such a time and place for the Mormon people." (Heber J. Grant, remarks at the dedication of the Winter Quarters Monument, 1936.)

A person who has no vision may draw from this

pioneer experience what appears to be an obvious conclusion: families perished. But in an eternal perspective, they did not. It was their willingness to sacrifice everything—even life, if necessary—that would ensure the salvation of these families eternally.

Gordon B. Hinckley, in a talk to students at Brigham Young University in March 1972, said, "The family is the center of all things. We had the family before we had the gospel. The purpose of the gospel is to eternalize the family unit, to make it operative in the eternities to come as well as in this life, for it is in the home that most of the problems of this world will be settled, not in the federal government, the U.N., or any other organization."

The patriarchal order, designed for the government in the kingdom of God, is simple and perfect. It places parents with family members in a position of accountability for their own direct family kingdom. It requires willing compliance to the laws of God. The Prophet Joseph Smith taught, "God has in reserve a time . . . when He will bring all His subjects, who have obeyed His voice and kept His commandments, into His celestial rest. This rest is of such perfection and glory, that man has need of a preparation before he can, according to the laws of the kingdom, enter it and enjoy its blessings. This being the fact, God has given certain laws to the human family, which, if observed, are sufficient to prepare them to inherit this rest. This, then, we conclude, was the purpose of God in giving His laws to us." (*Teachings of the Prophet Joseph Smith*, p. 54.)

Under the patriarchal order, there are boundaries, not barriers. There is structure, but each member of the family must be free to act on his or her own in accordance with correct principles, strongly influenced by family values, and with the well-being of others in mind. When parents and children are taught this divine concept of the eternal family unit and understand and accept it, they have a basis for all of their decisions. They simply ask, "Will this action move

us closer toward our goal or delay our progress individually and as a family?"

Even when we possess clearly defined goals and an
understanding of the law, we will be challenged as we try
to make the plan work in the daily routine of life. One well-
meaning parent determined to establish some family rules
or laws. The scenario went like this: "Rule 1. Every child in
this household must be in bed and asleep by ten o'clock.
But if they are not asleep, they must be at least in bed by ten
o'clock. But if they are not in bed, they must be ready for bed
or at least in the house thinking about getting ready for
bed. OK, they must at least be in the house so I can go to bed
by ten o'clock."

The majority of families in the United States and in
many other countries no longer live in rural settings as in
the past. In an urban society, the efforts of children are gen-
erally not essential to the welfare of the family; they do not
work side by side with parents to provide the basic needs
for survival. No longer are family values discussed regularly in prolonged conversations at mealtime and during
the household chores. No longer are members of the
extended family—aunts, uncles, and cousins—living in
close proximity and available to reinforce, reward, and
rejoice together in daily family happenings.

Today many families are splintered by conflicting work
schedules. Family mealtime is irregular, if at all, and
microwave ovens and fast foods have robbed us of mealtime rituals. A study of first graders' reading readiness
found that "high scorers had a radically different atmos-
phere around the meal table," as compared to the low scorers. The former group enjoyed family meals that were "a
focus for total family interaction" and were both positive
and permissive in emotional tone. ("The Family in
America," The Rockford Institute Center, p. 3.)

Consider the effects of current lifestyles and of increasing affluence on a growing sense of isolation. In a society in
which family members often have separate bedrooms,

individual television sets, and video players and earphones, individuals tend to become more independent, which can contribute to feelings of loneliness, rejection, and despair. Incidences of abandonment, abuse, neglect, and emotional aloofness also occur, and use of drugs and alcohol and reports of suicide increase. In the absence of communication and time spent together, families often experience a diminishing of shared values.

The factors that dim the vision of the sacredness of the family unit are varied and numerous. In the early 1970s, media ranked eighth as an influence in the lives of teenagers. By 1988 it ranked second—and was battling with parents for first. Much of what we see in the media today tends to distort and even destroy the values associated with the ideal family. In a recent survey of television programs on a Salt Lake City channel during a twenty-four-hour period, researchers counted eighty-six incidents of immoral conduct, eighty-eight portrayals of violence, and forty-five uses of vulgar language. And in an article entitled "Television as a Value Setter," we read: "Schools don't dare impose values. Parents are busy and confused themselves. And organized religion plays a smaller part in many people's lives. There has been an erosion among the traditional suppliers of values." (*TV Guide,* July 23, 1988, p. 5.) According to a study by the National Institutes of Mental Health, adults and children alike use TV to learn how to handle their own family roles.

The media and retail stores present choices designed to create in consumers insatiable desires that can never be satisfied, resulting in a hungering that is out of control. A decade ago, the average supermarket carried 9,000 items; today it carries 24,000 or more items. Marketing campaigns feed people's appetites, particularly those of youth, as though identity, acceptance by peers, and personal worth can be found in brand names. These economic and social pressures impose devastating problems for families.

The types of entertainment people engage in today are

becoming increasingly passive, resulting in more isolation and less socializing of family members. Video parties, loud music, and costly public entertainment present few opportunities for interpersonal communication.

While societal forces are working to create a great gulf between the vision of the family and the realities of the environment in which we live, the family does continue to be recognized as a critical factor in our society. One magazine writer observes: "Throughout history nations have been able to survive a multiplicity of disasters, invasion, famines, earthquakes, epidemics, depressions, but they have never been able to survive the disintegration of the family. The family is the seedbed of economic skills, money habits, attitudes toward work, and the arts of financial independence. The family is a stronger agency of educational success than school. The family is a stronger teacher of the religious imagination than the church. . . . What strengthens the family strengthens society. . . . The role of a father, a mother, and of children . . . is the absolutely critical center of social force. . . . If things go well with the family, life is worth living; when the family falters, life falls apart." (Michael Novak, "The Family Out of Favor," *Harper's,* April 1976, pp. 42–43.)

Truly, where there is no vision, the family perishes. But when the promises of eternity press upon us daily and we train our appetites to hunger after the things of the spirit, we can live in the world without being a part of it. We know where we are and what our families' challenges are. We have a vision of where we want to be and what the rewards are. Our responsibility is to make decisions that will move us from where we are toward our ultimate goal of exaltation.

As the world ripens in iniquity and the family continues to be under increasing attack, the family unit need not perish. Individuals within each family can survive. Families can be together forever. A refuge can be created and preserved. Our homes can be our safe places. But we must be constantly alert to guard against the termites of contention that are infesting our safe places, going about their destructive work behind the scenes with relentless tenacity. The guidelines are clear. The path is straight. The promises are profound. But we must discipline ourselves, heed the counsel of our prophets, and abide the commandments of God.

President Ezra Taft Benson gives us this vision of the eternal nature of the family: "Adam and Eve provide us with an ideal example of a covenant marriage relationship. They labored together; they had children together; they prayed together; and they taught their children the gospel— together. This is the pattern God would have all righteous men and women imitate." ("To the Elect Women of the Kingdom of God," *Woman* [Deseret Book, 1979], p. 70.)

President Marion G. Romney said, "I feel certain that, if in our homes, parents will read from the Book of Mormon prayerfully and regularly, both by themselves and with their children, the spirit of that great book will come to permeate our homes and all who dwell therein. The spirit of reverence will increase. Mutual respect and consideration for each other will grow. The spirit of contention will depart. Parents will counsel their children in greater love and wisdom. Children will be more responsive and submissive to the counsel of their parents. Righteousness will increase. Faith, hope, and charity, the full love of Christ, will abound in our homes and lives, bringing in their wake peace, joy, and happiness." (*Ensign*, May 1980, p. 67.)

The family council can provide the basis for establishing and maintaining close family relationships and open communication. According to President Benson, family councils imitate a heavenly plan. (See *Ensign*, May 1979, p. 88.) They can help family members work, play, and grow together, become more sensitive to the needs of others, and set goals and evaluate progress. The 1989 Relief Society manual (p. 170) stated, "Family councils also establish habits of communication and mutual respect on which both children and parents can rely when serious and difficult problems arise within the family or in the lives of individual family members."

A Home Front radio message sponsored by the Church notes that "the average family talks together less than five minutes a day." Communication is essential to the survival of the family, but it must be done in an attitude of accepting, appreciating, and valuing changing behavior. Human beings are dynamic, ever changing, and in the process of becoming. Thus, the challenge of effective communication is that it is never fixed. Accepting constant change increases an attitude of expectation, tolerance, and excitement about the process. There is no simple, easy way to communicate. Part of the joy of living comes from working through the process. And when families spend time together in an environment that invites trust, their communication becomes more effective, and the effects extend far beyond the family circle.

In a recent attitude survey, teenagers were asked if they could change one thing in their lives, what would it be? The highest desire for most of the respondents was to be able to change their family relationships. They wanted to be able to talk to their parents as they talk to their friends about important matters. Yes, teenagers often behave in unexpected and unpredictable ways that may frustrate and alarm their parents. But too often children are rejected just when they need the greatest support.

Conflict results when parents think of children as they were and as they should be, not as they are and as they are becoming. It is difficult for many parents to allow their children to leave childhood behind and to become more independent, thinking adults. But the process of "becoming" is vital and exciting. When changing, growing teens are accepted, they can contribute immeasurably to the family unit. Perhaps the role of the parent should be one of more teaching and less preaching, more listening and less lecturing, more discussion and fewer demands, more praise and less punishment.

Elder L. Lionel Kendrick of the First Quorum of the Seventy has reminded us: "Our communications are at the core of our relationships with others. If we are to return home safely to Heavenly Father, we must develop righteous relationships with His children here in mortality. . . . Christlike communications are expressed in tones of love rather than loudness. They are intended to be helpful rather than hurtful. They tend to bind us together rather than to drive us apart. They tend to build rather than to belittle. Christlike communications are expressions of affection and not anger, truth and not fabrication, compassion and not contention, respect and not ridicule, counsel and not criticism, correction and not condemnation. They are spoken with clarity and not with confusion. They may be tender or they may be tough, but they must always be tempered. . . . Christlike communications will help us to develop righteous relationships and ultimately to return to our heavenly home safely." (*Ensign*, November 1988, pp. 23–24.)

The preservation of the family unit requires time. Each day we must decide on our priorities for that day and how much time we will spend in working on those priorities. The report on "The Family in America" observed: "Middle class children who are placed first in their parent's allocation of time and attention show superior academic skills when compared to children who receive less attention. Quantity of time, not quality, appears to be the central variable. Relative to verbal achievement, for example, it is not selective training and skills but a close time-intensive, ongoing relationship between the mother and the child that is critical." For children, spending time together with parents and sharing feelings are of greater worth in building confidence and faith than are material things.

The eternal welfare of the family begins with the marriage covenant between a man and a woman. This covenant creates a family. The children become an extension of the family unit. Concerning decisions of marriage and related responsibilities, President Benson has said, "Some of our sisters indicate that they do not want to consider marriage until *after* they have completed their degrees or pursued a career. This is not right. Certainly we want our single sisters to maximize their individual potential, to be well educated, and to do well at their present employment. You have much to contribute to society, to your community, and to your neighborhood. But we earnestly pray that our single sisters will desire honorable marriage in the temple to a worthy man and rear a righteous family, even though this may mean the sacrificing of degrees and careers. Our priorities are right when we realize there is no higher calling than to be an honorable wife and mother." (*Ensign*, November 1988, p. 97.)

This may not be the blessing for all women at this time. Some of us live with unfulfilled expectations concerning our families in this life. But it is an unwavering conviction of the eternal nature of the gospel plan that keeps the vision of family ever burning brightly.

Some years ago a young Lamanite woman attended a university where I taught. Recently she sent me a letter in which she shared how her vision has guided her decisions and her life: "I was a new member in a small Lamanite branch with about twenty friendly people. Seven were from my family. That year [the year of her baptism] was a turning point in my life. Having been baptized and with a burning testimony, I knew answers would follow my questions. My vision of life and its purpose became clearer each day. Even as a student in junior high, I knew I wanted to graduate from seminary, high school, and college, be married in the temple, and have a family. I did not know exactly what the future held, but above all I absolutely knew that the two most important goals were temple marriage and family. I never lost sight of this vision despite the struggles, challenges, and options along the way. . . . When making decisions, especially major ones, I'd pray and then ask myself, 'What effect will this have on a temple marriage, family, and eternal happiness?' This was my model question in youth and is even today as an adult. By asking myself this question when making decisions, I do not lose sight of the vision I have of Heavenly Father's plan for me."

She achieved her goals of graduation from high school and from college and went on to earn a master's degree. She received many honors, including a Presidential appointment, worked on several national boards, and obtained a position with one of the world's largest computer companies. Shortly after that, she was sealed in the Mesa Temple. She writes: "I have recently made another important decision. I have decided to leave the company so that I can concentrate on motherhood. Some of my friends are surprised; others pleased; while others respond with, 'You are what? Rarely does anyone leave the company.' The important thing is I feel good about my decision. Yes, I will leave a fine salary, professional development, the excitement of travel and nice friends in the company, but all of that is so minor when I ponder the meaning of eternal happiness and to seek first the kingdom of God.

"Gone are the IBM titles, recruiter specialist, education specialist, and community relations specialist. In the near future I am planning on a major promotion, 'mom specialist.' As I think of that new title, my face beams with a big smile and I immediately experience a feeling of inner warmth and peace. I feel so good about my latest decision to put my career on hold. For me, making important decisions is accompanied by prayer, a momentary reflection of eternal purposes, and pondering of scriptures. Having an eternal vision is critical to making good decisions. I have tried to make these decisions with a vision of Heavenly Father's plan for me. These very decisions have made all the difference in my life."

Where there is no vision, the family perishes. But if the

vision is clear, even in the most difficult times, and we are on course, we can join with our brothers and sisters who have gone before us singing, "All is well; all is well." Our Eternal Father will renew our vision daily as we seek Him in prayer. He reaches His arms to us to assist us in our crossings over the chasms of life. He will be there to welcome us with our families.

Chapter 11

Relationships: A Sacred Triangle

In the musical *Fiddler on the Roof*, Tevye one day anxiously presses his wife, Golda, for something he yearns to know. "Golda," he says, "do you love me?" Somewhat surprised, she responds, "Do I what?" Tevye repeats his question: "Do you love me?"

She answers, "You're a fool."

"I know, but do you love me?"

"I'm your wife."

Again he presses. "I know, but do you love me?"

Golda then lists all the things she does for him, as though that were statement enough. Yet Tevye, needing to secure the relationship, puts the words in her mouth: "Then you love me."

Almost as though by discovery, she responds, "I suppose I do."

Tevye finally risks expressing his own feelings and says, "And I suppose I love you too."

Then together they sing, "It doesn't change a thing, but even so, after twenty-five years, it's nice to know."

In a marriage relationship, it is so nice to know.

Another relationship in which feelings of love were expressed is that of Thomas Moore, an Irish poet, and his wife. When he returned from a business trip, he found that his beautiful wife had locked herself in her upstairs bedroom and asked to see no one. She had contracted smallpox, and her complexion was now marked and scarred. After looking at herself in the mirror, she demanded that the shutters be drawn and that she never see her husband again.

Thomas Moore did not care about the smallpox and went to her room. She asked him to leave. He went off by himself, and that night, though he had never written a song before, he not only wrote the words of a song, but also composed the music. Early the next morning he returned to his wife's darkened room. "Are you awake?" he asked. "Yes," she said, "but you must not see me." "I'll sing to you then," he said. He sang to his wife his song, which still lives today.

> *Believe me, if all those endearing young charms*
> *Which I gaze on so fondly today,*
> *Were to change by tomorrow and fleet in my arms,*
> *Like fairy gifts fading away,*
> *Thou would'st still be adored as this moment thou art,*
> *Let thy loveliness fade as it will,*
> *And around the dear ruin each wish of my heart*
> *Would entwine itself verdantly still.*

The song ended. Then Thomas's wife crossed the darkened room to the window, slowly opened the shutters, and let in the morning light.

Unconditional love that is expressed can bring light where there is darkness, and replace sorrow with hope and even joy. All relationships in marriage are to be tried and tested as two lives become blended into one, as they become "one flesh." (See Matthew 19:5.) A marriage relationship that is growing is also changing. When we are changing, we have to continually adjust to change and work out new challenges.

Love is learned, and until it is learned and felt and expressed unconditionally, we can have times of loneliness. As Albert Schweitzer says, "We are all so much together and yet we are all dying of loneliness." The marriage relationship can remove feelings of loneliness, but it requires time and concern for each other, a sharing of feelings.

We are all familiar with the phrase "If you love 'em, tell 'em." "I love you" are three small words, and on occasion they may be thoughtlessly repeated from habit. But when they become linked to precious time spent together, when a couple see into each other's hearts and listen and care and share, the three words blossom into full-length messages. Even without hearing the words, we listen with the heart instead of the ears: I know what you are thinking, and I love you. I know what you are feeling, and I love you. I know what you are doing, and I love you. I know what you are not doing, and I still love you. I know you, and I love you.

Early in a marriage, a couple run the risk of feeling that if one of them has a different opinion from the other, one is right and the other is wrong. While it is important that each person be at one with the other, feelings of confidence and self-worth can be undermined if one partner always has to let go of his or her ideas as wrong. There must be unity without sacrificing identity.

In time a couple learn that they have choices about how each will respond in those inevitable times of differences. One of the important discoveries is to learn that one of them doesn't have to be right all the time. This frees that individual to be right some of the time. I can be right, and you can be right. We can both can be right. There can be two rights.

It is easy in a relationship, especially in times of stress, to focus on things that aren't right instead of on all those things that are right. We can lose perspective and let little things irritate our relationship and even destroy the precious things.

After we walk the road together for a distance, the little things that may have been annoying become the sweet and precious things that we cling to with inexpressible fondness. We learn to look at both sides of the coin and give thanks for one and laugh at the other. She says, "The qualities I love in him are his commitment, his firm determination, his unwavering faith, and his strong will for righteousness. I love him most for his stalwart strength in times of storm. Yet, why do I get so annoyed with what seems to be a stubborn streak on occasion?" And he says, "I love her for her sensitivity, her beauty of thought, her tenderness, her responding to the subtle beauties that others might overlook. I love her for her compassion and tenderness and the hurt she feels at others' discomfort. Yet why am I annoyed at what seems to be an oversensitivity when I am brisk or impatient?"

When we talk disagreements out together, bonding takes place. A relationship is tried and tested in times of disappointment, discouragement, and maybe even despair. But when we link arms and tread the way to God, hand in hand, the valleys that we traverse together can bring us to the mountain peaks. Marriage relationships are tempered and welded in times of adversity. Volumes have been written on the process of building strong relationships, but experience tells us that success depends not so much on a formula that we follow as on a commitment to each other that we feel. With that commitment, we work through the barriers that could be destructive and use them as bonds to strengthen, stabilize, and weld heart to heart, and soul to soul. Then privately we go about our secret ways to bring joy to each other.

As we spend time with each other, we will begin to open up and share what is deep within our hearts so that we really get to know each other and stay close. Our relationship will determine the safety of our home and determine whether our home will become a refuge from the world or a battleground.

When we leave the security of our home, we may find ourselves battling the complex pressures of society, and on occasion we may return with battle fatigue and wounds. Our home can be a first-aid station where wounds of all kinds are healed. Expressions of love, like manna from heaven, need to be gathered every day. Love isn't something we store up. We draw it fresh from God each day. The love that we express can feed the soul of both the one who gives and the one who receives. It can become a message of power to transform lives because in expressing true love, we must dip into the reservoir of divine love, the love of Christ. We share in part the pure love of Christ, the fountain of all love.

In the relationship between husband and wife, as perhaps in no other relationship, we find this statement applicable: "Thee lift me, and I will lift thee, and we will ascend together." What does that mean?

In our marriage, my husband and I discovered early that we had strong differences of opinion on some things. Our backgrounds were different, our perspectives were different, and in some cases our interests were different. But our values and eternal goals were the same. It is in our sameness that we continue to build our relationship, not in our differences, although our differences have added to the breadth and depth and richness of our relationship. This insight often comes after years of molding, testing, giving, and sharing.

May we invite you into our hearts and share with you one of our special husband-and-wife relationships.

It was Christmas Eve. The magic of Christmas seemed more real that year, not so much because of lights and tinsel, but because we had a feeling of excitement from the inside out. Family members had gathered at our house for our traditional dinner. Then Grandpa gathered us in the living room, opened the Bible, and read once again the Christmas story from Luke.

After the stockings were finally hung and treats left for Santa, the children reluctantly, yet eagerly, went to bed. They tried hard to get to sleep while listening intensely for any sounds from the expected night visitor.

"Now, if Heber would just go to bed, I could finish my

gift for him," I said to myself. I had been working on this gift for my husband for about three months, and I needed about three more hours to complete it. But despite my encouragement for him to leave the room, he kept lingering. It was evident he would wait for me. I decided to go to bed and wait until he dropped off to sleep; then I'd slip out and finish his present.

With the lights out and the house quiet, I lay in bed looking into the dark, too excited to sleep. I listened for his heavy breathing, which would let me know it was safe to slip away. To my amazement, after a little while he whispered, "Ardie." I didn't respond. A conversation now would only delay the time when I could finish my project. To my great surprise, when I didn't answer he slipped out of bed as cautiously as I had planned to.

"What is he up to?" I wondered. I couldn't get up then. I waited and waited, but he didn't return. What should I do? Maybe if I went to sleep, I could awaken at about three o'clock and finish my project before everyone got up at about six, the time Grandpa Ted had agreed that we should all gather around the tree.

I was aroused from sleep when Heber got into bed ever so quietly. Only a few minutes later, his heavy breathing assured me he was sound asleep. It was three o'clock.

Months earlier, we had talked about Christmas and made the traditional gift list that ranged from the ridiculous to the sublime. At the top of my list was a wish that we could have more time together so he could teach me his great understanding of the gospel. I was driving two hours each day to BYU, and his schedule was very busy. Our time together was precious.

Heber's list of wants was short, as usual, but he did express a concern for the responsibility he had as a stake president to lead the way for his stake members, and it bothered him that his family history was not compiled. His family group sheets were incomplete.

My gift to him was finally wrapped. I could hardly

believe I had done it, but there it was—the evidence of many hours of work. I hurried back and slipped into bed just in time to hear children's voices from the other room. "Grandpa says it's time to get up. Hurry! We can't wait!" they said. Neither could I.

In the living room Heber handed me a package. I opened it and found a box of cassette tapes. On top of the box was a message: "My dear Ardie, While you are traveling each day, I will be with you. As you know, the Doctrine and Covenants has been of special interest to me over the years. I have enjoyed reading and recording for you the entire book. Reading it with the purpose of sharing it with you, I have endeavored to express my interpretation and feelings so that you might feel what I feel about this sacred book. I finished it only a few hours ago. May these tapes add to your wisdom and help unfold the mysteries of God and prepare us for our eternal life together."

Then I handed Heber my gift. He tore off the wrapping, and inside was a book of remembrance—many pages of pictures and stories never before recorded, a result of secret trips to visit and interview relatives and the assembling of records and histories.

On the first page of the gift was a message: "Dear Heber, As I have copied, reviewed, and prepared these sheets and interviewed family members, your ancestors have become very real to me, and I have an increased appreciation and understanding of the greatness and nobility in the man I married. Although I never met your father, and met your mother only once, when I meet them I know I'll love them and know them better because of this gift I have prepared for you, which really has been a gift for me."

I don't remember any of the other gifts we received that year, but Heber and I will never forget the spirit of that glorious Christmas celebration.

Looking back now to that time so many years ago when

we knelt at a sacred altar in the temple and clasped our hands in an eternal triangle, we realize that we have had more than a companionship. We are not two but three— thee and me and God for eternity, a most sacred triangle, a relationship of which we are each a part.

Chapter 12

Just the Two of Us—for Now

My husband and I do not have any children at the present time. Our blessings in this matter have been delayed. But make no mistake, we are even now a family. Our family unit was established by the authority of God at the same time that we knelt at the altar in the temple. Children come as an extension and expansion of the family. When a man and a woman are married, they immediately become a family and remain a family even in the temporary absence of children.

I mention this because I know many young couples struggle with the sorrow of childlessness. I would like to share with those who have not been blessed with children my testimony and some of my insights gained from personal experience about our particular challenge. Because these experiences are so personal, I have seldom shared them outside the walls of our own home.

Heber and I understand and remember some of the pains and much of the suffering that we endured. We remember the emotional highs and lows with every month, including the fast and testimony meetings when testimonies were borne by those who asked in faith and were blessed with children. We know how it is to return home and put two dinner plates on the table and to recall the marriage covenant to multiply and replenish the earth, and to desire desperately to qualify for that honor in righteousness. We know how it is to not be able to explain our feelings to each other, much less to family and friends; and how one's whole soul cries out as did Job, "If I be righteous, . . . I am full of confusion; therefore see thou mine affliction." (Job 10:15.)

Some go through the suffering and concerns of childlessness year after year until finally they may even say, "My soul is weary of . . . life" (Job 10:1), thinking that if they have no children, they cannot fill the measure of their creation. And if they don't fill the measure of their creation, they may say to themselves, what else matters?

I will forever remember the day a child new to our neighborhood knocked on our door and asked if our children could come out to play. I explained to him, as to others young and old, for the thousandth time, that we didn't have any children. This little boy squinted his eyes in a quizzical look and asked the question I had not dared put into words, "If you are not a mother, then what are you?"

But then came the day my young husband was called to be a bishop and I was finally convinced that our not having children was not because of our unrighteousness. Some don't understand that. A good man in the ward who had desired the position to which Heber had been called came to him privately and said, "What right do you have to be a bishop, and what do you know about helping a family? Don't ever expect me or my family to come to you for anything!" In time my husband helped that man's family through a serious crisis, and through it we forged a lasting bond of love with them.

Others have undoubtedly had similar experiences. Mother's Day may be one of those times of hurt. Every year there will be a Mother's Day, and every year at church a little plant or some other gift may be forced into the clenched fist of the woman who has not had a child. But one day she will learn to open her heart, and then, somehow, she will open her hand to receive that gift. Eventually, that gift becomes the symbol of an eternal promise. In these ways we grow from the time when everything hurts and offends us until, with faith in God, we are neither hurt nor offended.

I know a childless woman who, at the age of fifty-eight, went into the hospital for a hysterectomy. She couldn't handle the emotional impact of that event, and she wept bitter tears of anguish, saying, "Now I know that I'll never have any children." She and her husband lived together in loneliness, waiting, never facing reality and never able to make the adjustments that could have brought them a full life.

How do we handle unfulfilled expectations? First, we must accept the reality that this life is not intended to be free of struggle. In fact, it is through struggle that we are given opportunities to fulfill the very purpose of this mortal life. It is the fiery trials of mortality that will either consume us or refine us.

Part of those trials is facing alternatives and making decisions. For those of us without children, the choices may seem incredibly difficult to make. What would the Lord have us do? To what extent do we seek medical attention? What about adoption and foster children? What about no children—and if that is the choice, then what do we do with our lives? The choices are never simple. During these times of searching, we often find ourselves caught between conflicting counsel from parents and friends and leaders and doctors and other experts. Some couples I have known even consider divorce, each one thinking the other is responsible.

From my own experience, I've learned that the only lasting peace is the peace that comes when we learn the Lord's will concerning our opportunities in life. To do that, we must consider our alternatives, formulate a decision, and take it to the Lord. Then, as President Dallin Oaks observed when he was president of Brigham Young University, "When a choice will make a difference in our lives— . . . and where we are living in tune with the Spirit and seeking his guidance, we can be sure we will receive the guidance to attain our goal. The Lord will not leave us unassisted when a choice is important to our eternal welfare." (*Brigham Young University 1981–82 Fireside and Devotional Speeches* [Provo: University Publications, 1982], p. 26.) I believe that. We just don't know the Lord's timeline, and that is where our faith comes in.

I have two younger sisters, both of whom are mothers. My youngest sister, Shirley, has eleven children. Sharon, another sister, has a little girl who was born to her after six years of anxious waiting. Ten years later, through the fervent prayers of the extended family for the wonderful blessing of adoption, a little boy came into their family and was sealed to them in the temple for time and eternity. What a blessing he and the other children have been to all of us!

Over the years my sisters and I, with our husbands, have prayed for each other and with each other and about each other. We have come to know that the Lord has answered our prayers differently and not always in the affirmative and not always according to our timeline. But we have all felt the warm assurance of His approval and love.

There will be times when we may feel that our desires are righteous, but the answer is still no. At that point, the only way to peace is to say, "Not my will but thine be done." The Lord doesn't have to explain His decisions to us. If He did, how would we learn faith? I have learned that we must make our choices—even the hard ones—and then accept responsibility for the consequences. It is in facing the awesome responsibility of using our agency and, in faith, making decisions of great eternal consequence, that we are drawn close to God.

Someday, maybe years after the trial of our faith, we will receive a witness that our decisions were right. (See Ether 12:6.) But until then, those who try to live in tune with the promptings of the Spirit must exercise no small degree of faith and courage in following that Spirit.

What, then, are some of the decisions couples can make to lead fulfilled lives when the answer is that they will not have children in this life? One night, as my husband and I were reaching for that kindly light to lead us amid the encircling gloom, we read a statement from President David O. McKay: "The noblest aim in life is to strive . . . to make other lives . . . happier." (*Conference Report,* April 1961, p. 131.)

These words were like a beacon in the dark. They became a motto, a guiding light. That night, speaking, I think, by inspiration from the Lord, the patriarch of our family said to me, "You need not possess children to love them. Loving is not synonymous with possessing, and possessing is not necessarily loving. The world is filled with people to be loved, guided, taught, lifted, and inspired."

My husband and I knew that parents are constantly placed in situations that help them develop unselfishness and sacrifice. We began to realize that if we were to learn the important lessons that our friends with children were learning, we needed to place ourselves in situations where we could serve and sacrifice. So we began to say yes to everything and to everyone.

It wasn't long before we had many opportunities to serve and sacrifice. Often, at the end of a long week we would plan for a moment together—just the two of us—and the telephone would ring. We'd postpone our moment together and carry on with joyful, grateful hearts for our opportunities, hoping to qualify even in some small measure for the quality spoken of by Elder Neal A. Maxwell: "So often our sisters [and I would add brothers] comfort others when their own needs are greater than those being comforted. That quality is like the generosity of Jesus on the cross. Empathy during agony is a portion of divinity! . . . They do not withhold their blessings simply because some

blessings are [for now at least] withheld from them."
(*Ensign*, May 1978, pp. 10–11.)

We who do not have children can wallow in self-pity—
or we can experience "birth pains" as we struggle to open
the passageway to eternal life for ourselves and others. I
bear testimony that instead of wrapping our empty and
aching arms around ourselves, we can reach out to others.
As we do so, one day we can even be able to hold our
friends' babies and rejoice. We can rejoice with the mother
of a new bride, and the mother of a newly called missionary, and even with our friends the day they become grandmothers. How can that be? Let me tell you.

We were alone with each other at a motel in St. George,
Utah, one Thanksgiving time when all our relatives were
with their families. Early in the morning, I lay in bed thinking. I remember my heart crying out as I anticipated
Christmas approaching. And although we could share in
the joy and excitement of our nieces and nephews, it wasn't
like having our own children with stockings to hang. The
whole thing seemed to me to be unfair. I felt darkness and
despondency settle over me, and I did what I had learned
to do over the years. I got on my knees and prayed for
insight.

My answer came when I opened the scriptures to
Doctrine and Covenants 88:67–68: "And if your eye be
single to my glory [and remember, God's glory is to help 'to
bring to pass the immortality and eternal life of man'
(Moses 1:39)], your whole bodies shall be filled with light,
and there shall be no darkness in you; and that body which
is filled with light comprehendeth all things. Therefore,
sanctify yourselves that your minds become single to God,
and the days will come that ye shall see him; for he will
unveil his face unto you, and it shall be in his own time, and
in his own way, and according to his own will."

I don't know how long it will be for others who have
similar longings. For us it was years. But one day we did
gain an eternal perspective, and we felt peace, not pain;

hope, not despair. I would have liked so much to have received that insight years before, but I know that had that happened, I would have been deprived of the growth that comes from being comforted by the witness of the Spirit after the trial of my faith.

If I have any comforting message for others, it is this: Peace of mind comes from keeping an eternal perspective. Motherhood, I believe, is a foreordained mission. For some, this glorious blessing may be delayed, but it will not be denied. Motherhood is an eternal reality for all women who live righteously and accept the teachings of the gospel.

On the other hand, the characteristics of motherhood, which include concern for others, sacrifice, service, compassion, teaching, encouraging, and inspiring, can be the noble labor for each of us now, with or without children. The fate of each spirit in the eternities to come depends so much on the training it receives from those here and now who are willing to help another gain eternal life.

To participate in this glorious work gives meaning and purpose, great joy, and eternal blessings each and every day, even as we anticipate the promises of the future.

If that does not give enough comfort, let me close with this thought by President Brigham Young:

"Let me here say a word to console the feelings . . . of all who belong to this Church. Many of the sisters grieve because they are not blessed with offspring. You will see the time when you will have millions of children around you. If you are faithful to your covenants, you will be mothers of nations . . . and when you have assisted in peopling one earth, there are millions of earths still in the course of creation. And when they have endured a thousand million times longer than this earth, it is only as it were the beginning of your creations. Be faithful, and if you are not blest with children in this time, you will be hereafter." (*Journal of Discourses* 8:208.)

Chapter 13

All Kinds of Mothers

As my mother and I sat quietly listening to the many praises expressed in beautiful music and tender words, I glanced at her graying hair and her thin hands folded together in her lap, a white handkerchief bordered with lace tucked between her fingers.

It was Mother's Day, and the program, while it had followed the traditional pattern, seemed especially inspiring this year. The personal examples given as testimonies of true motherhood were expressed by persons of all ages. We were taught by the Spirit as each speaker expressed tender feelings of the heart. I felt a reverence for life itself, and an increased awareness of my debt of gratitude to the mother sitting beside me—she who, over the years, had experienced many challenges, blessings, and rewards, and some heartaches, each leaving in its wake evidence of the aging process so much a part of this mortal life. Just a few short years ago Mother was a child herself, and then a wife and mother, and now a grandmother. And the wheel turns ever so quickly.

With trembling hands she now graciously accepted a small pot of pink begonias, as did each mother up and down the rows. As she sat holding this small token of appreciation, I heard again in my mind the comment she had made when we entered the chapel. Half to herself, yet audible to me, she had said, "You know, I don't like

Mother's Day. It always reminds me of the things I could have done and didn't." Then she added, with a serious note, "I hear about the ideal mother and wonder how my children have done so well."

While the little plants were presented to each mother, I wondered about the praises so generously given. Were they as readily accepted? Or were some held in reserve in the minds of many mothers for those who they thought were more deserving?

The question of eligibility for such honors might be raised as a mother thinks back on those times of stress when her own children emphatically declare that someone else's mother is more understanding, more trusting, and certainly more patient, even though she knows that those very times might be evidences of greater love that qualify her for the honor. And so it is that mothers of all ages may see themselves falling short of that ideal which they would hope might one day be within their reach, little realizing that at that very moment they stand on the threshold of greatness. The self-recorded ledger, which might otherwise reveal an excess of assets, may appear lacking because the recording is incomplete. It is in the heart and soul of the child, and not the ledger kept by the mother, that the record of her labors is more accurately recorded, just as the epistles of Christ were "written not with ink, but with the Spirit of the living God; not in tables of stone, but in fleshy tables of the heart." (2 Corinthians 3:3.)

Years ago the president of a large company gave the following account: "I remember, when I was very young, a mother with three children who had very little in the way of worldly goods; on birthdays and other special days the most she could do was to give her children a small toy made with her own hands. However, she always did something else which in my mind was worth more than the most expensive toy ever made. On a child's birthday she would call him into the bedroom, sit him down in a chair, and then kneel down to pray. In her prayer, she would thank her God for blessing her with this child, and she would enumerate the pleasures that the child had given her, and pray for his continued health and happiness. . . . I can only express my personal opinion, but I do believe that there are many children today who have very expensive toys, but who would trade them all for such an experience." (*Fedco Reporter*, June 1957, p. 25.)

I wonder if the magnitude of that experience went unrecorded except in the life of the child.

And what of the mother whose little second grader, in the midst of snickering from his classmates, stood tall and responded to the teacher's inquiry as to who might like to be a neighbor to cross old Mr. Black in the story they had just heard. The boy's mother was unaware of her teaching recorded in the heart of her child, a teaching that rippled out to everyone in the class, as her son looked first at the teacher, then at the children, and said with conviction, "I wish Mr. Black was my neighbor, because if he was my neighbor, my mom would bake a pie for me to take to him. Then he wouldn't be that way anymore." Another child responded, "I wish I'd said that." And a mother's labors were recorded in the "fleshy tables of the heart" of her child and others.

Another mother, maybe at the expense of clean windows and polished floors at home, stood in the hallway at school waiting to retrieve the frozen salmon she had taken from the freezer that afternoon and brought to school so her son Ernie could give a report on fish. She could not possibly have made an accurate recording of her labors that day because she did not witness the miracle she had wrought while standing in the hall waiting.

Ernie had been a child with little confidence, bashful and insecure among his classmates, but that day, as he stood in front of his class, all eyes were on him, for he held in both arms against his chest a thirty-six-inch salmon. His classmates were enthralled when he told them how he and his dad had caught this great fish in the Columbia River.

From that day on, it was different for Ernie. The students thought that if he could fish, he could do anything else. Instead of being last, he was now chosen first. Instead of sitting alone, he was the center of attention and everyone wanted to sit by him. He was still Ernie, but in his own quiet way he began to unfold like a butterfly emerging from a cocoon.

Something of a miracle had taken place. This mother had been about her labors, and yet when she returned to her less than orderly home that day, she might have wondered if she had accomplished anything, since the evidence of what had not been done was so apparent.

My sister Shirley, with her family of young children, described the routine schedule of her day as one crisis after another in constant regularity. One problem in this family was the habit of leaving bicycles in the driveway. According to a decision made in family council, those who left bicycles in the driveway were subject to punishment; they were to be grounded for a week.

Glancing out the kitchen window one day, Shirley saw the familiar sight—two bicycles in the driveway. It was this teaching moment that loomed more important than any other, if her children were to learn the language of the Lord through the scriptures and find the solutions to childhood problems in gospel principles.

Calling her son Lincoln to her side, she explained, "Lincoln, Jennifer has left her bike in the driveway. What do you think we should do? Should we ground her or give her another chance?" Without remembering his own negligence, he spoke in defense of his younger sister. "Oh, Mom, give her another chance. She just forgot. Give her one more chance and I'll help her remember."

Dismissing Lincoln, she then called Jennifer to her side. "Jennifer," she said, "Lincoln has left his bicycle in the driveway. What do you think we should do? Should we ground him or give him another chance?" Jenny, free-spirited and always quick to respond, did not hesitate.

"Ground him," she said. "That was the decision. Ground him."

A different answer might have required less time, but the time for this lesson was now. Calling both children to her side, Shirley said, "Lincoln, if you will take your bicycle out of the driveway immediately and put it away, we will give you another chance." Lincoln looked somewhat surprised and relieved, since he had been unaware of his own offense. Jennifer, then remembering and looking a little anxious, awaited her own instruction. Placing one arm around her little girl, her mother said, "Jennifer, my dear, we will need to ground you for a week, according to the family decision." To this seemingly unfair treatment Jennifer immediately resisted. And then from the scriptures lying open on the kitchen table, frayed and worn, their mother read to them from Matthew 7:2: "For with what judgment ye judge, ye shall be judged: and with what measure ye mete, it shall be measured to you again." Time was allowed for questions and for answers to whys, until even Jenny felt secure about the great confidence her mother expressed in her as she spoke of her unusual gifts and talents and her radiant personality that needed a little tempering. And so by the end of the day this young mother was, as usual, probably behind in many things, but way ahead in others.

With so many illustrations for comparison, how easy it would be for a mother to suffer a sense of inadequacy while she reflects on all the things she didn't do—without remembering or in some instances even being aware of all she did do.

I don't ever remember my mother taking hot cookies out of the oven when I came home from school. But I do remember working alongside her, stocking the shelves of our country store, and how she treated every customer with the same respect—the immigrants, the wealthy grain growers, the Indians, the neighbors, the friends, and the children. "Everyone," she said, "deserves to be treated with dignity," and she showed me how.

I don't remember that she taught me to sew, but I remember something of compassion and charity as I would see her put into a box of groceries for a needy family items that she never wrote on the bill. I don't remember her sitting with me while I practiced the piano, but I do recall many a child coming to our store with a penny to make a difficult selection from all the different candies available, and Mom waiting patiently while the decision was made and then often changed even after the candy had been dropped into the sack and the top of the bag twisted.

Now, years later, sitting by her side with a host of precious memories flooding my mind, I wondered if my mother suffered a little as she resisted the praises intended for her (though none seemed to fit our situation exactly) because she had tutored her young using a somewhat different approach.

To suppose that nurturing, tutoring, and mothering should be the same for all children is folly. A fable tells of the animals who organized a school at which, to make it easier to administer the curriculum and evaluate progress, every animal was to take the same subjects. According to the fable, "the rabbit started at the top of the class in running but had a nervous breakdown because of makeup work in swimming. The eagle was a problem child and was disciplined severely. In the climbing class, he beat others to the top of the tree, but he insisted on using his own way to get there. The prairie dog stayed out of school because the administration would not add digging and burrowing to the curriculum." The very skills and gifts that made each one great individually were being overlooked through a curriculum designed for blanket applications to everyone.

It is with spiritual insight and consideration of the eternal plan that the praises for motherhood take wing and fall on those women otherwise not considered for such an honor. Is a mother born only with the birth of her child? Is motherhood reserved only for those who give birth? Was not the sacred mission of motherhood foreordained by God for all women before the world was?

This lesson came to our family on Tuesday, December 19, 1978, when the telephone rang at 2:15 in the afternoon in my sister's home. A voice spoke these brief but penetrating words to my brother-in-law: "We have a baby for you, just three days old. You and your wife may pick him up at four o'clock." A flood of telephone calls followed. Excitement, anxiety, adjustment of schedules and plans, neighbors and friends and relatives running in with emergency supplies of clothing and bedding and bottles—and the whole neighborhood seemed to stand at attention in honor of this glorious event.

It was not until eleven o'clock that night that my husband and I were able to pay the newborn an official visit. All was quiet. The lights of the neighboring homes were now darkened, and only a dim light shone through the glass panel by the door as we tapped lightly and tiptoed in. There, in the love seat, with the flickering light from the fire and the soft lights from the Christmas tree casting a glow over this blessed occurrence, sat the little family: the father on one side and the mother on the other, with their arms entwined across the back of the couch, and tucked securely between them was little Shelly, now nine years of age, an only child until today. Nestled in a soft flannel blanket in her arms was her little baby brother, his head resting on her shoulder, his dark hair contrasting with her long golden curls.

Without words to distract from the sacredness of this moment, Shelly, looking a bit pale from the late hour and the emotional excitement, wiggled forward to the edge of the couch and stood up. Tenderly cradling the wee baby in her arms, she gently laid him in my arms, never taking her eyes from him until she looked up to exclaim, "I'm a real sister now!"

In that moment I witnessed not only a sister, but a real mother with her mission beginning to unfold—the gentleness, the tenderness, the caring and protection all displayed in such perfection. The baby made a sound and the child responded as a weld of spiritual oneness was felt—spirit responding to spirit. Was not the reality of motherhood inherent in the child? And what of Shelly's mother—although she did not give birth to this baby, was she not giving life and light, and demonstrating motherhood in a most divine way?

I have come to know that we can all rejoice in the sacred calling of motherhood. To give birth is only one part of this sacred mission, the miracle of life. But to help another gain eternal life is a privilege that is neither denied to nor delayed for any worthy woman. And to be a mother in Israel may be within reach of every righteous woman even now.

Motherhood is a holy calling, a sacred mission for carrying out the Lord's plan, that of nurturing the body, mind, and spirit of each of those who kept their first estate and came to earth to be proven in their second estate, "to see if they will do all things whatsoever the Lord their God shall command them." (Abraham 3:25.) The fate of each spirit in the eternities to come depends so much on the training it receives by those who honor motherhood and that sacred trust.

Maybe it is an awareness of the magnitude of this divine stewardship and its eternal consequence that causes mothers, including my own, to consider with soberness the acceptability of their performance. And yet, we do not have to be perfect in this life to receive eternal rewards. These rewards and honors so much deserved are not reserved. They are to be conferred now on your mother and mine, and on all who are striving to bring eternal life after birth to any one of these little ones.

While the ledger may appear wanting in the eyes of some mothers, our Father in heaven hears the prayers of their children, His children, who speak in behalf of their mothers and reveal much more than the record might show. A few years ago, at age six, my niece Shelly gave a remarkable accounting of her mother's stewardship when she prayed, "Heavenly Father, I'm thankful I have a Mom to make a red skirt with pockets and a Dad to read the Book of Mormon when Mom can't. I'm thankful that you and Jesus are up there and that we have temples to get married in and for Nephi that wrote the Book of Mormon."

And even the record kept by a child bears witness of labors not recorded by the mother, yet with eternal consequences. From two journal entries of my friend Becky Smith, just eleven years old, we read:

"*July 15, 1978:* Mark and Kevin were riding bikes when they saw two swallows swoop down so they stopped. It was a robin (less than a month old). The two parents had been killed by a cat so they buried the parents and brought the baby to me! So I am now the mother to a baby robin. We don't know if it will live since it doesn't have its true parents but I hope so!!! We got it on the 15th."

"*July 16, 1978:* My poor little robin. It's so sick. We gave it a blessing and I'm staying home from church. I was holding it in its little blanket when it looked up at me as if to say, 'Thank you for trying to help me,' and closed its dear little eyes for good. I buried it in a gold box under my rose bush. I'm very sad but where it is I know it is safe and I hope to see it in heaven. I know it is happy and that God will take care of it."

And then a final entry for that day: "My Mom and I went to the mountains to get some wild flowers. It was fun. She is a great great comforter."

Because of her mother's part in that happening, recorded in the heart of the child is increased reverence for life, for birds, flowers, and mountains, and for all of God's creations. Her mom, her "great great comforter," reached out to the tender feelings of her child.

And that reaching out by mothers continues day after

day as one month follows another while the years slip by. Her caring is continuous and even increases at those times when the opposing forces are most threatening.

Because of what is recorded in the hearts of the children by those who carry out their foreordained sacred mission of motherhood, I believe words similar to these will one day be heard: "Come, ye blessed of my Father, inherit the kingdom prepared for you from the foundation of the world. For you nurtured my spirits and helped them to keep their second estate, so that they might have glory added upon their heads for ever and ever."

And many righteous women will probably answer, "But when did I help prepare them? What did I do?"

And the response will be heard: "You baked a pie for your little boy to take to Mr. Black. You took a salmon to school. You took care of the bicycle in the driveway my way, and taught your little ones charity and patience. You went to the mountains and picked wild flowers. You knelt with your child in prayer. You stayed steady in times of trouble and storm. You made red pockets for your little girl's dress.

"And inasmuch as you have done it unto one of the least of these my children, you have done it unto me."

Part IV

We Learn as We Live

Chapter 14

The Joys of Teaching

It was a matter for immediate attention, some discussion, and a little humor when the editor picked up what appeared to be a slight error while proofreading a catalog listing. The new manual (which was to become a valuable resource for teachers throughout the Church) was listed in the catalog as "Teaching, No Great Call." Was it possible that just two missing letters could make such a difference in meaning? No time was wasted in making the simple correction. The accurate title now read "Teaching, No Greater Call."

While this error was quickly resolved, a much more difficult and important challenge would be to make the same correction in the heart and mind of anyone having the impression that teaching is "no great call." Yet that serious error does exist. "Just a teacher," some say of their involvement professionally, in the Church, and even in the home. And with that thought, seeds of attitude are sown that, like heavy clouds on a sunny day, cast a dark shadow over what might otherwise have been a glorious time of teaching from dawn till dusk.

Instead of teaching being "no great call" as some may think, instead of it being "just a job" in the minds of others, the understanding of the joy that accompanies the sacred trust to teach is reserved for those who discover that teaching is more than a job. Teaching extends far beyond the responsibility to disseminate information, facts, theories, and knowledge. That alone makes teaching a job. But it is usually as one is absorbed in instructing that the joy of teaching bursts open like fireworks exploding into magnificent flashes of color, illuminating the heavens. Similarly, the student, while persistently struggling through the darkness in the quest for learning, suddenly experiences a glorious burst of insight and knowledge.

For Jeff there were hours and hours of constant encouragement by his teacher while he tried to understand for himself the difficult process of long division. Page after page of newsprint was covered on both sides by "just one more try." Jeff, with his teacher's help, continued the struggle to unlock the door that would allow him to learn this process. Tuesday passed. Wednesday melted into Thursday. On Friday, in the late afternoon while his classmates were quietly reading their favorite books, Jeff finally released from his worn-down pencil onto his very smudgy paper some numbers that for the first time, for him, made sense. In an explosion of ecstasy he burst forth with words never before spoken by this timid yet persistent child: "Hey, I'm not dumb after all!" Everyone looked up, and for the teacher, at least, it was like beautiful, colorful fireworks bursting forth in a darkened sky.

On another day Julie squinted her eyes with her little face turned upward as if trying harder to hear and understand what the teacher was trying hard to explain. The teacher's voice was becoming a little more intense as she tried yet another way to explain what she had already gone over several times before. I was Julie's teacher, and with little experience in teaching, I began to feel very worried about my responsibility to this child. It was as I stood anxiously over her—observing her shoulders leaning forward, her head lowered close to the page, the firm grip on her pencil, and her tireless efforts to keep trying—that the real impact of team teaching flashed into my mind. I paused a moment and pleaded silently, "Father, help me teach this child who is thy child. Don't let her confidence slip while I struggle to master the art of unlocking doors. Allow me to learn the ways of the Master Teacher while I share in this sacred responsibility of teaching one of thy little ones."

With that immediate and constant access to the ever-present resource of a divine "team teacher," I tried once again. This time the key turned and the door swung wide. "Finally you said it right!" was Julie's jubilant outburst. Her broad smile and increased confidence were reward enough for the time it took to finally "say it right."

Even the most difficult, sometimes disagreeable, and even heartbreaking job of teaching can be transformed into the joy of teaching when we begin to grasp the eternal nature of such a call. Elder John A. Widtsoe gave a wider perspective to our understanding:

"In our pre-existent state, in the day of the great council, we made a certain agreement with the Almighty. The Lord proposed a plan conceived by him; we accepted it. Since the plan is intended for all men, we became parties to the salvation of every person under that plan. We agreed right then and there to be not only saviors for ourselves, but measurably saviors for the whole human family. We went into a partnership with the Lord. The working out of the plan became, then, not merely the Father's work and the Savior's work, but also our work. The least of us, the humblest, is in partnership with the Almighty in achieving the purpose of the eternal plan of salvation." (*Utah Genealogical and Historical Magazine,* October 1943, p. 289.)

If we have "so much the advantage in the world to come" because of the knowledge and intelligence we have gained in this life through our diligence and obedience (D&C 130:19), then surely anyone who assists in any way in contributing to a person's knowledge, reassuring him in his diligence, and encouraging him in his obedience becomes a teacher "in partnership with the Almighty in achieving the purpose of the eternal plan of salvation."

Bodies are born only once, but many rebirths take place as teachers gently and reverently lead their students to discover their own gifts and endowments, talents and abilities so generously bestowed by a divine Father, for which the student is steward. It is in understanding the eternal nature and the divine potential of the material with which a teacher is entrusted that she leaves her imprint in the human clay that transforms a routine job to inexpressible joy.

Teachers are allowed, on occasion, to assist their students in unlocking the door to a vault of eternal talents, talents that at times have been locked up too long by those suffering from feelings of inadequacy, discouragement, and lack of faith in their own ability and in their own divine potential.

In the fall of the year, a young woman was completing her student teaching in a third-grade class. She had been diligent in learning the mechanics and methodology, and by the standards of the academic world was an excellent teacher. Yet, in her heart she felt no joy of teaching; rather, hurt and often nagging discouragement and lack of confidence, like spreading aphids on a rosebush, were sapping her strength and hampering her growth.

We sat together at the close of the school day. The classroom was quiet, the children gone. The smell of chalk dust filled the air, adding a heaviness to the silence that seemed to be closing in. "I can't do it," she said, her eyes filling with tears. "I just can't do it." I knew of her great desire to be a good teacher and her untiring efforts to succeed, yet her confidence was so weak that she saw everything she did as less than acceptable. She had gradually convinced herself that she was doomed to failure and there was no escape.

The curriculum for this important moment had not been provided. As I listened to her, I felt myself reaching out, pleading for an answer. A thought began to unfold, and I found myself posing questions—not so much about her performance, but about the children's increased achievement because of her efforts in teaching. Was not Sarah doing better in spelling than she had done even a week ago? What did it mean to have the children crowd around her desk during recess and ask for "just one more song" as she played their favorite tunes on her guitar and sang with them? Had not a child raised his hand indicating a need for help, a need to which she responded? On the playground that very day, had not her voice blended with the cheering that brought Jimmy home safely in the winning home run? Had she not opened doors for children—many doors, doors that in some cases might even have remained closed, at least for a time?

Her troubled countenance softened slightly, with the hint of a smile. It was in discovering the evidence of others' progress that she began to discover her own. During the following weeks she spoke more often about what was happening to the children in her class and less often about what was happening to her. The disruptive worry about her own inadequacies seemed to be gradually slipping away as she recognized her ability to help others. Some weeks later I received a letter from her. "What do you say to thank a person who has helped to change your life? You've pointed out to me things that I always thought were just part of me, instead of bad habits that could be changed. I know it's going to be a long process, but I know that if you've got confidence in me, I can do it. Thank you for a new life. You are the vehicle by which it was sent. Love always."

It is only through team teaching that the inspiration for some lessons can be realized, allowing the teacher and the student to be taught. "And now, if your joy will be great with one soul that you have brought unto me into the kingdom of my Father, how great will be your joy if you should bring many souls unto me." (D&C 18:16.)

Into the sacred realms of another's heart, the teacher must proceed reverently, with deep respect, and teach clearly and forcefully truths to which the Spirit can bear witness. President J. Reuben Clark stated: "The mere possession of a testimony is not enough. You must have besides this, one of the rarest and most precious of all the many elements of human character,—moral courage. For in the absence of moral courage to declare your testimony, it will reach the students only after such dilution as will make it difficult if not impossible for them to detect it; and the spiritual and psychological effect of a weak and vacillating testimony may well be actually harmful instead of helpful." ("The Charted Course in Education, "*J. Reuben Clark: Selected Papers on Religion, Education, and Youth* [Brigham Young University Press, 1984], p. 250.)

It is not in knowing perfectly the twenty-third Psalm and then teaching with great skill the meaning of each word that a teacher experiences the ultimate joy. It is, rather, in coming to know the Shepherd and then reverently guiding another person to that same knowledge. Only then is a teacher privileged to take part in His work, which is also our work.

The sacred mission of teaching and the ultimate joys that attend—those most lasting, those felt most deeply—are often borne out of struggle, anxiety, and determination that is sustained only through unwavering faith in God. The moments of greatest anxiety can become forerunners to the deepest joy and ultimate ecstasy when a mother teaches her own child. In the inspiring example of Ruth Yancey, as she has dedicated her life to teaching her children, and especially her son Steven, I witnessed evidence of this great joy borne out of struggle.

In the first few days after Steven's birth, Sister Yancey and her husband began suspecting something might be wrong with their precious baby, although he had gained several pounds since his two-pound eleven-ounce birth weight. An ophthalmologist confirmed the young couple's grave concern. Heavy doses of oxygen used to save his life were more than the tiny blood vessels of his eyes could stand. Those blood vessels had ruptured, and he was blind.

One morning after her husband had gone to work, Sister Yancey cradled her son close to her and began pleading with the Lord. "Help me to know how to teach him, what to say, how to show him so he can accomplish each task," she prayed. "Inspire me, because I am your tool in teaching this special spirit. I'm weak. I'm uneducated. I'm unknowledgeable about what should be done. Help me to know what to do and how Steven and I can accomplish it."

With faith in God, this dedicated mother willingly and anxiously shouldered the responsibility of teacher and walked carefully into those first fundamental lessons. "We thought that when children got teeth they'd know how to chew," she said, "but they don't. Children learn from imitation, by seeing others chew. So I would put food in my mouth and place his little hands on my jaws and chew. Then I would put food in his mouth. He would spit it out or start to choke, but after a while he began to learn how to manipulate his jaws." Months later she realized the joy of that first accomplishment—he had learned how to chew.

When her son was just a little older, this faithful young mother had to prepare for other lessons, one after the other. "In teaching Steven to walk, I couldn't say, 'Walk to your daddy,' because he couldn't see his daddy. So we bought a little push toy for him that we called his lawn mower. He learned to walk with that. He wouldn't dare walk around the house without it, because he was afraid he would bump into something."

While the lessons were very difficult for the child, it was his mother who had to be willing to suffer if the next hurdle were to be crossed.

"When Steven was two years old," she continued, "we built a fence around our backyard so he would have a protected area to play in, and I would feel more secure about his safety. The plan was good only for a while, until the day when he found his way to the gate. Day after day he would stand at the gate and cry."

Sister Yancey told how she and her devoted husband together found the strength to do what had to be done. They bought Steven a little toy truck with a steering wheel and a seat. When he sat on the truck his feet touched the ground, and he could "walk-ride" the truck down the sidewalk. This provided something he could hold onto and something that would be ahead of him and protect him from falling in case of interference in his path.

"The first few times I would open the gate and let him out on the sidewalk alone, then go into the house and watch the clock. I would tell myself that I must not check on him for two full minutes. I would force myself to let him be gone for two long minutes at a time, then I would run out to see if he was still on the sidewalk and going in the right direction. Then I would go back into the house and wait another two full minutes."

Gradually, with faith, the teacher's confidence in herself and her child grew. Steven would go to the end of the block and turn around and come back. In time it was two full blocks. Without the struggle required to open the gate, the rewards and victory might have been withheld, to the detriment of mother and child.

In the events of those very early years, there were also moments of great joy. About two months after Steven's second birthday, the Yanceys moved into a new home. Steven and his four-year-old brother, John, were playing in the living room while their parents were busy putting things away. Suddenly Brother and Sister Yancey heard "America" being played on the piano. Both came running into the living room. "We thought John must be playing the piano. But it was not John. We just stood there. It was like a miracle. This baby for whom we had concerns about brain damage, his hearing, his sight, and all those kinds of things, was playing 'America' in octaves with his third fingers resting on the tops of his index fingers on both hands just to get enough strength to play the notes."

From then on young Steven could duplicate on the piano the melody of any music he heard. He played hymns, nursery rhymes, popular music. By the time he was four or five he could play almost anything, but still just in octaves. "Whenever I played the piano he would climb up on my lap and lightly place his little hands on each of my arms so it didn't restrict me at all, but he could feel the movement of my playing. It was so easy to teach him music, whereas most of the things I taught him were quite a struggle. We worked; we had frustrations; we both had tears. Sometimes we wondered if we were going to make it—like the effort to help him learn to tie his shoes—but teaching him music was a joy."

When Steven was a little older, his parents, anxious to provide maximum opportunities for him, purchased a second piano. Sister Yancey, an accomplished musician, would sit at one piano and he would sit at the other. "No matter what I would play, how big the chord, or how long the phrases, he would always be just a split second behind me. He would learn it and memorize it as we would go. His mind is like a tape recorder; once a piece is there, it is not forgotten."

During Steven's senior year in high school, he took a class in music history and composition in which he had to orchestrate a song. He chose "Sunrise, Sunset" from *Fiddler on the Roof*. He wrote the parts for all the instruments in a full band—twenty different scores. Together Steven and his mother discussed the characteristics and voice range of each instrument. He would experiment on the piano until he could decide what he wanted each instrument to do. Then he would dictate that part to his mother, and she would transcribe it on staff paper. Together they would transpose it to the key of that instrument. "With his ear, having perfect pitch, and my eyes, we made a pretty good team. I couldn't have done that without him and he couldn't have done it without me. What a thrill it was when the Viewmont High School concert band played it for us. There have been many such times of great joy."

Graduation from high school presented more challenges. The ceremony was to be held in a very large auditorium on a circular stage. "Steven wanted to walk across that stage by himself. His father and I helped him work out a way this could be accomplished. We took him to the auditorium. The custodian told us which ramp the graduates would be using, and where they would leave the stage. So Steven and his father and I counted the steps from the end of the carpeted ramp over to the table where he would receive his diploma, and from there over to the other ramp. We walked through it together many times. His dad would guide him up the ramp, Steven would walk the full width of the stage unhesitatingly by himself, and I would be there at the other ramp to receive him. This way Steven would be getting that diploma all by himself."

The graduating class that year was large, and the conducting officer requested that there be no applause. Well, there was no applause until they announced Steven's name—then the whole senior class stood up and applauded. Steven not only received his diploma, he also received a college scholarship in music. "It was one of the proudest and happiest moments of my life," his mother said. "It really was."

For a young bird, pushed gently from the security of the nest, there comes a time for the solo flight, when the teacher must stand in the wings trusting that the teaching has been sufficient for the immediate challenge, and wings are spread in flight and there is no turning back. It was at the airport that Steven made final preparations for his solo flight. His mother and father, brothers and sister would remain behind. He had accepted a call to serve the Lord on a two-year mission to the Anaheim California Mission. Steven grabbed the handrail and made his way carefully into the big jetliner that would take him away to unfamiliar places. "As he left my side I got such a feeling of peace," his mother recalled. "It was that feeling of putting him into the hands of the Lord, as the Lord had put him into my hands. I had done my best, and now I knew the Lord would care for him."

Instead of waiting for two full minutes after opening the gate, this trusting mother was prepared, with peace in her heart, to wait two full years with less anxiety than the two full minutes had previously demanded. Much, much learning had taken place. "I feel pride in him, and sometimes pride in myself that I was able to help him. But that is secondary. The most important thing is the feeling of gratitude, even to the point where I'm grateful for those hard things to learn and to teach. Life could be easier and more pleasant if we didn't have struggles, but we don't grow much that way." This great teacher expressed her joy and gratitude by saying, "I'm thankful I've had the chance to cope with things I would not have chosen to cope with because we've all learned so much."

The Yanceys are still learning and striving and serving as they share their talents and gifts with others. At a recent concert presented by Steven and his mother, the attentive audience filling the hall waited with almost a sense of adoration while this saintly mother, refined through struggle, guided her handsome young son to the grand piano. She then moved quickly to the organ some distance away and took her place. The entire audience seemed to be wondering just how these two performers would begin together the very difficult classical selection that Steven had announced as their first number. After a brief second of anticipation, the whole auditorium was filled with the beautiful tones of piano and organ in perfect unison.

Later Sister Yancey smiled as she confessed, "It may have sounded as if we began precisely together, but actually I was just a split second behind him. That's the way we work—he goes first and I follow." Her explanation sounded almost like an echo of years gone by when she spoke of Steven's efforts as a five-year-old. She had explained then, "No matter what I would play, he would always be just a split second behind me." But there was a difference now. He went first, and the teacher's work was glorified through another.

It was the Master Teacher who opened the gate, allowing each of us to learn the lessons, even the difficult ones, that would ensure our continued growth and give us the opportunity to reach our divine destiny. He marked the way and invited us to follow. As we feed His sheep, we are drawn most closely to Him and feel His nearness through the joy of teaching.

Chapter 15

The Book of Mormon:
Letters from Home

I have a little set of scriptures that my mom and dad gave me when I turned seventeen. I had read the Book of Mormon before, but one day it was different. Perhaps I was more in tune with the Spirit or maybe I had studied more diligently and prayed more fervently. I was young, but I wanted to know for myself if the Book of Mormon was true.

On that particular day I came to the part about faith in the thirty-second chapter of Alma. As I finished that chapter, I experienced a feeling that I recognized as a witness from the Holy Ghost. I knew the Book of Mormon was true. I wanted to stand up and shout. I wanted to tell the whole world what I knew and how I felt, but I was alone. So, with tears of joy streaming down my face, I wrote on the margins, all the way around the page, the feelings in my heart at that moment. I made a big red star in the margin on top of the page and wrote, "May 31st, 7:30 A.M. This I know, written as if to me." Then I wrote in the margin on one side of the page, "I have received a confirmation. I know the Book of Mormon is true!" Across the margin on the other side of the page I wrote, "One month ago I began fasting each Tuesday for a more sure knowledge. This I know."

I am anxious for you—my neighbor, my sister, my friend—to know and love the scriptures so they can be a comfort when you climb the steep and scary and risky trails of life. When I read the Book of Mormon, I feel as if I am getting letters from home from my Heavenly Father, who is guiding me with inspiration in the important choices I must make each day. When I consider how much I love the Book of Mormon and how frequently I turn to it for guidance, inspiration, encouragement, confidence, and increased faith, I wonder sometimes if my great love for this book might have been passed down to me by my great-grandmother.

Almost a century and a half ago, a copy of the Book of Mormon was brought into the home of Susan Kent, my great-grandmother, when she was sixteen years of age. After studying the book, Susan gained a testimony of its messages that was so strong that she could not reject it, although to accept it meant a great sacrifice for her.

At the time Susan was engaged to a young man, and she felt that she could not endure being separated from him; but he would have nothing to do with anyone who would join the Mormons. She did not stop to count the cost. She chose the path of peace for her conscience. However, her heart was so grieved that she could partake of no nourishment for several days. She lapsed into a coma so profound that it had the appearance of actual death. Preparations were being made for her funeral when she awoke asking, "How long have I slept?" With tender care she slowly regained her health, and she and her sister, Abbegale, and their parents joined the Church. I will be eternally thankful to Susan Kent for her testimony of the Book of Mormon and what it meant in her life and now in mine.

Just a few years ago, our bishop called me to his office and asked me if I would accept the calling to chair a committee that would encourage every young person in our ward to read the entire Book of Mormon within the next seven months. At that time my aged mother was in extremely poor and failing health. Late one evening as I sat by her bedside, I pondered the bishop's challenge. Something about the spirit of that evening, with my mother's life hanging in the balance, caused me to think about eternity and the importance of this life and how quickly it passes. I reflected on the important messages of the Book of Mormon and wondered how the other youth leaders and I might motivate young people to experience reading these sacred scriptures in such a way that each one of them would gain an unwavering testimony or at least the beginning of a testimony.

Together we did a lot of planning and praying. Ten of the young people were called and set apart as "captains of ten" to direct the program we devised, which we called "The Moroni's Promise Project." We launched this program at a special meeting on a Sunday evening. That was a memorable Sunday for me, for that very morning, as if to test my own commitment to the Book of Mormon and to this program we were about to begin, my mother passed away. At our meeting that evening many testimonies were borne and commitments were made. For me, it was a special opportunity to pay tribute to my mother and the inspiration I had received concerning the Book of Mormon while sitting at her bedside.

That was a glorious year, as young people read and reported, read and reported. Seeds were planted and testimonies were strengthened. Some began reading for the first time. One young captain, Michelle Gardner, reminded us of a promise President Gordon B. Hinckley made to all members of the Church who read the Book of Mormon: "There will come into your lives and into your homes an added measure of the Spirit of the Lord, a strengthened resolution to walk in obedience to his commandments, and a stronger testimony of the living reality of the Son of God." (*Ensign,* November 1979, p. 9.)

As the young people reached the end of the book of

Alma, they each received a T-shirt imprinted with the letters "S.T.O.M.P." The letters stood for "Students Trying Out Moroni's Promise." They were well on their way to finding the reality in the promise of Moroni, chapter 10, verse 5.

For those who completed their reading of the Book of Mormon, the letters "S.T.O.M.P." took on even greater meaning. They learned that a testimony of the Book of Mormon will "stomp out" discouragement. It will "stomp out" feelings of loneliness. It will "stomp out" lack of faith. It will "stomp out" disobedience. It will "stomp out" anger. It will "stomp out" despair.

How does the Book of Mormon do all this and much, much more? As we read and study these inspired scriptures, the Spirit touches our hearts and we come to know and to love our Lord and Savior, Jesus Christ. Our awareness of His infinite love for us increases. We learn about the atonement and how, through the ordinances and covenants of the gospel, our Father in heaven has provided a way by which we can qualify ourselves for all of the blessings He has in store for those who are obedient. We learn how to repent, how to forgive, and how to love one another as our Savior loves us. With intense desire, we come to want to be like Him and to one day be with Him. We gain greater understanding of the purposes of this life and why we need to be tried and tested. And we learn to walk by faith.

My testimony of the Book of Mormon is not only what I know in my own heart, but what I have witnessed in the hearts of others, such as the valiant youths who accepted our bishop's challenge, as the Book of Mormon has become a part of their lives. The Book of Mormon is the anchor to my faith. I thank my Heavenly Father for it and for my testimony, which is my most priceless possession. My greatest desire would be that every woman, young and old, throughout the entire Church—yes, even the world—will study and pray about the truth in the Book of Mormon and gain a personal testimony for herself of this great gift that God has given us.

Chapter 16

Confirm Thy Soul in Self-Control

The last line of the third verse of "America the Beautiful" has an important message for each of us: "Confirm thy soul in self-control." What does this mean? I believe it means having harmony and unity within us, which provides agreement between our spirit and the desires of the flesh. It means having inner strength and inner peace because we have accepted responsibility for ourselves and developed controls that make us whole.

Self-mastery is a continual process. Sometimes we wish it were easier than it is, and at times the very lessons that provide the greatest growth are the ones we would like to avoid, or at least to ignore, if possible. For example, one day my niece, who was practicing the piano, became very exasperated while going over a difficult part of her assigned piece. Finally, with both hands resting heavily on the keys, she said, "Mom, it's too hard!" Her mother, in an effort to encourage her, said, "My dear, just try that little segment five more times. . . . No, Mom, not five," was the response. Her mother, wanting to place the responsibility where it belonged, said, "All right, my dear, you decide." "No, Mom," my niece said, "you decide—but don't choose five."

Sometimes we, like this budding little musician, would

like to shift the responsibility for our actions to someone else, or we find excuses for how we feel or how we react. Often we have conflicts that we need resolve. We don't want things to be too hard for us, but still we want to reach our goals. On one hand we have good goals and want to be pushed to meet them. On the other hand, we resist change. We are not sure that we want the struggles that come with bringing ourselves from where we are to the goals we want to reach.

Growth is often painful. It requires letting go of the old and reaching for new heights. Someone has said that "if fate would destroy a man, it would first separate his forces and drive him to think one way and act another. It would rob him of the contentment which comes only from unity within." Our thoughts and our actions have to be in harmony. I believe that it is in confirming or securing our souls in self-control that we find ourselves, that we discover who we really are.

May I share an eternal truth that has helped me to better understand not only our opportunity but also our responsibility to gain self-control, or self-mastery. In the Doctrine and Covenants the Lord tells us, "The spirit and the body are the soul of man." (D&C 88:15.) If we are to each confirm our soul in self-control, it will come as we experience the process that puts the spirit in control over the physical body. We need to know what we are trying to control. There is often a battle going on while our spirit struggles to get control over our body and overcome desires of the flesh.

When we set goals and don't reach them, make personal commitments to ourselves and don't keep them, we experience the sensation of battle fatigue. Why is this so? President Brigham Young taught: "The spirits that are in men are as pure as the gods are. Then why do they consent to do evil? Because of the influence of evils that are in the flesh. When mankind gives way to evil and suffers the flesh to rule and contaminate the pure spirit tabernacled within it, the spirit within does not answer approvingly. Although the inhabitants of the earth are in darkness and blindness, yet they are not so ignorant as they represent themselves to be. There is a spirit in them that reproves them continually when they do wrong."

Thus, if fate would destroy us, it would cause us to think one way and act another, causing the spirit to be in conflict with the desires of the flesh. When we live with integrity, as the Young Women Value states, we make our actions consistent with our knowledge of right and wrong. Gaining self-control is a gradual process. It comes as we have repeated experiences that demand the spirit to reign supreme.

A simple illustration of this principle can be observed in an experience I had at a girls' camp a few summers ago. It was late at night and the girls were all in their sleeping bags. The lights had been turned out except for one flashlight in an upper bunk. I got out of my sleeping bag and climbed up on the bunk to check on Becky, who was sitting there with her flashlight under her arm, working on a little piece of handiwork with yarn and a needle. I asked, "Becky, what are you doing at this time of night?" "Making a pillow for my mother," she said. "Her birthday is next week." I noticed on the side of the canvas little pieces of brown yarn at ten-row intervals. She explained, "If I do ten rows every day between now and then, I'll have it ready in time." I could see there was no possibility of diverting her from her goal, so I encouraged her to continue while I went back to my sleeping bag.

But I didn't go to sleep immediately. I lay in the dark and wondered about this pillow. Suppose Becky were to go to sleep after completing eight rows and then did twelve tomorrow? Or, considering the coldness and the inconvenience of using her flashlight, couldn't she finish the pillow when she got home? It wasn't until I took my mind off the pillow and thought of the pillow-maker that I got an insight into the greatness of what was going on. After the pillow will be long forgotten, the experiences that were being woven into this young woman would last forever. It was the discipline of the pillow-maker that mattered most. The pillow was not of any eternal consequence, but the process of setting goals and being in control was.

The next day I was thrilled when I observed what I considered a transfer of self-mastery from one area to another. Becky was at the head of all of the others as we climbed up the steep mountain. She was also the one who responded when help was needed in the kitchen. She wasn't lagging behind; she was out in front. The confidence she had in herself seemed to say, "I can do it," and the reward for such discipline gave her exhilaration for life and new opportunities. I think this is the very concept that President Kimball was encouraging when he said, "I believe in goals, but I believe that the individual must set his own goals. Success should not necessarily be gauged by reaching a set goal, but by progress and attainment."

Each of us has a rendezvous with destiny, a mission in life. There is an urgency that we be responsible for the progress we make every day. We must avoid the danger of being lulled into a loss of precious time by allowing ourselves to think that days and seasons will return again and again and are recycled through our Monday, Tuesday, Wednesday; January, February, March; winter, spring, summer, and fall. There will be other Fridays and there will be other springs, but not this particular one. This day lost will never return, nor will the opportunity of this day. While our daily duties and sometimes our tiresome tasks and laborious labors may not seem of eternal consequence, what happens to our spirit as we labor is of eternal consequence. Living the gospel won't protect us from the trials and tests, but it will help us to grow from them as we master how we will respond to circumstances.

What is this power we seek that puts us in control of ourselves? It is much more than will power. Will power comes and goes. We get it and we lose it for a time. No, what we seek relates to spirituality, spiritual power that comes when we strive to be totally obedient to all of the laws of God and make Christ the center of our life. In Isaiah, we read, "They that wait upon the Lord shall renew their strength; they shall mount up with wings as eagles; they shall run, and not be weary; and they shall walk, and not faint." (Isaiah 40:31.)

In the song "America the Beautiful," the last line of the third verse concludes, "Confirm thy soul in self control, thy liberty in law." Liberty and freedom come from obedience to divine law. Unfortunately, our society today has done much to supplant self-control and encourage disobedience to divine laws. Through artificial means and the use of drugs, we can control almost any physical or emotional need. We can be pepped up or tranquilized. We can escape the feelings of hunger through diet pills. Moral laws can be broken with seemingly considerable protection from any responsibility. Many people actually escape life while they live it, willfully fleeing the realities of their life's mission, thinking that control in other areas compensates for lack of control within.

With every law, there is a blessing. It is through obedience to a specific law that we receive a specific blessing. When we understand the law and the blessings, we can better discipline ourselves to abide the law. As we strive to live in complete harmony with the laws of God, we are on our way to self-mastery and to becoming more like our Savior. Obedience to the laws of God brings harmony within, happiness and peace; while disobedience to the laws of God brings misery, unhappiness, and disunity within. How we find ourselves in the morning and at noon and in the evening will depend upon our ability to confirm our souls in self-control. Sometimes we will experience battle fatigue, our spirits battling to control the desires of the flesh. For some the battle may be physical or social or spiritual or emotional—or even intellectual or financial, but we are all to be tried and tested so that we can grow.

Without developing self-control through a multitude of little victories, so to speak, we may never be prepared for the big tests and may never experience the liberty and freedom that come through abiding the laws of God. If we fail in the process of becoming totally responsible for our actions, we may find ourselves becoming more concerned with our daily conveniences than our eternal covenants, more attuned to our personal desires than our unwavering devotion. We cannot realize full joy because we will not experience necessary sacrifice. Our cannots become stronger than our commitments. We live the gospel casually but not devotedly. In the words of Julius Caesar, "The fault, dear Brutus, is not in our stars, but in ourselves."

I witnessed the joy and blessings of self-mastery at a Relief Society birthday celebration some time ago. It was a small ward, with a small gathering of sisters in the Relief Society room. After I gave my talk to the sisters about how we need to help each other on our way back home, I felt impressed to ask the young sister who had given the opening prayer to come to my side. Shaking, she stood beside me and I put my arm around her. I asked, "Is there anyone in this group who has really helped you on your way back home?" Her head dropped and she waited. I explained, "I suppose there are several, but is there one whom you could identify?" She looked up, her eyes moist, said, "Yes," and she called one of the sisters by name.

I looked over the small group and recognized immediately who that sister was. Tears were filling her eyes and moistening her cheeks. I asked her to join us at the front of the room, and she came up and stood by my side. I put an arm around her. Then I said to the first sister, "Would it be appropriate to ask how this sister has helped you on your way back home?"

She waited a minute, then looked up and said in a choked voice, "We worked in the Relief Society together over a period of time when we had a lot of misunderstandings,

some conflict and disharmony, and struggles in our relationship. Then one day we got together." Sensitively she
didn't say who initiated that coming together, but she
explained, "One day we got together and we talked
together. Oh, what I learned from her. I felt a change of feeling in my heart. For this understanding that came over me,
I will be eternally grateful."

I turned to the other sister and asked, "Did you know
she felt that way about you?" Tears were in her eyes and
she said, "No, I just knew I felt that way about her." My
arms were still around the shoulder of each of these sisters,
but behind my back I could sense that they were reaching
out to each other with arms entwined. I said to the audience, "Sisters, I want you to see what's going on behind my
back." Then I held these two women firmly, with one on
each side of me, and we turned around so other sisters
could see them in touch with each other. We then turned
back to the audience. "Don't let anything come between
you," I said.

I stepped back, and these two sisters embraced, tears
flowing freely, then took their seats. We all had been
touched by the Spirit because they had let go of their resent-
ment. They had taken control and allowed the Spirit to
overcome the frustrations and anxieties they had allowed to
build up.

Are you acquainted with the circumstances that surrounded the writing of the song "School Thy Feelings"? Let
me share it with you. Charles Penrose, who wrote the
lyrics, recorded the experience in his history: "This hymn
was . . . written for myself, about 1860, when I was in
Birmingham, England, before I immigrated. I had been
insidiously accused, not openly, but certain things had
been said about me and my presidency of the Birmingham
Conference [District], and particularly in relation to my
family affairs and possessions. . . . When I went to
Birmingham . . . I had taken a good deal of furniture and
stuff belonging to my family that did not belong to the

conference. It was intimated by one of the Elders from Zion that I was endeavoring [when reclaiming the furniture prior to moving] to lay claim to the property that belonged to the Birmingham Conference, and it touched me to the quick. I had labored then over ten years in the ministry, most of the time as a traveling elder, literally without purse or scrip. I started that way and had continued, suffering a great many hardships and difficulties and trials . . . and this touched me right to the heart. I did not know how to bear it. Weltering under these feelings I sat down and wrote that little poem, right from my soul." (Karen Lynn Davidson, *Our Latter-day Hymns: The Stories and the Messages* [Deseret Book, 1988], p. 323.) These are the words he wrote:

> School thy feelings, O my brother;
> Train thy warm, impulsive soul.
> Do not its emotions smother,
> But let wisdom's voice control.
> School thy feelings; there is power
> In the cool, collected mind.
> Passion shatters reason's tower,
> Makes the clearest vision blind.
> —Hymns, no. 336

A few years ago I had one of the most spiritual experiences in my life. My father, who was one of my dearest friends, was coming to the time of graduation—that's what he called it. He had stomach cancer, and over a period of time I witnessed literally the process of seeing what happens when the spirit is magnified and outgrows this mortal flesh. At this point he weighed less than one hundred pounds, his body almost gone. But his spirit was magnified to such refinement that to be in his presence was a spiritual experience.

Every day we would walk down a slight hill to the bridge about half a block from our home. A week before his graduation we walked down to the bridge once again. I had my arm around him to sustain him, and he had his arm around me to sustain me in the things that I needed.

As we walked down the hill, we looked out across the valley to the Great Salt Lake. The sun was shining down through breaks in the clouds, casting shadows on the lake. We stopped to rest on a little rock wall in front of a neighbor's house. Then this great spirit, one who had confirmed his soul in self-control, said quietly, "The world is so beautiful. It's been a good year."

"Dad, how can you possibly say that?" I asked.

In the same tone that he had often used to counsel me as a child, he said, "You can't ever look at one little part alone. You must see the whole picture. Just look at the beauties all around us. It's been a good year."

"Dad, how did you learn to always look at things like that?"

"Well," he said, "I had to learn to not let things bother me. It was I who had to determine how I would feel, not the circumstances around me. I learned I must be happy with the way things were for me." Then he repeated, "It's been a good year, Ardie, and a good life."

We made it to the bridge and rested, and then on the way back up the hill he reached into his unlimited reservoir of wisdom that he had memorized over the years and shared these lines: "I believe that God created me to be happy, to enjoy the blessings of life, to be useful to my fellow beings, and an honor to my country. I believe the trials which beset me today are but fiery tests by which my character is strengthened, ennobled, and made worthy to enjoy the higher things in life which I believe are in store for me. I believe that I am the architect of my fate. Therefore, I will be master of circumstances and surroundings and not their slaves. I will not yield to discouragement. I will trample them under my feet and make them serve as stepping stones to success. I will conquer my obstacles and turn them into opportunities."

Again we stopped for a little rest on the familiar rock wall. After catching his breath he continued, "My failures of today will but help to guide me on to victory on the morrow. The morrow will bring new strength, new hope, new opportunities, and new beginnings. I will be ready to face them with a brave heart, a calm mind, and an undaunted spirit. In all things I will do my best and leave the rest to the infinite." Then, with added emphasis, he concluded, "I will not waste my mental energy by useless worry. I will learn to dominate my restless thoughts and look on the bright side of things. I will face the world bravely. I will not be a coward. I will assert my God-given birthright as a man, for I am immortal and nothing, nothing will overcome me."

One spring I had an opportunity to stand on that sacred ground in Gethsemane and at Calvary, where we see the divine example of self-mastery. We read in James E. Talmage's book *Jesus the Christ* that it was customary prior to the crucifixion for the executioners to offer to the condemned person a narcotic drink for the merciful purpose of deadening his sensibility. When the cup was passed to Jesus, he was so much in control that he refused the drink. He was determined to meet even death with faculties alert and mind unclouded. In the hour of agony he prayed, "Father, forgive them, for they know not what they do." Only when his atoning sacrifice had been accepted by the Father and his mission completed did he bow his head and voluntarily give up his life.

As I stood in Gethsemane and then walked to the garden tomb, I thought, *He did all that for me, though he didn't have to. But he did. Whatever he asks, is it too much?* Then I pondered the thought, *Maybe it's not enough. Surely it's not enough.*

May we each confirm our souls in self-control and experience liberty—eternal, divine liberty—through obedience to God's laws.

Chapter 17

On Our Way
Back Home Together

Often as I address an audience, I am impressed with the realization that in all the history of the world, with the millions that have come and gone before us and those waiting in the wings, our turn on earth, yours and mine, is during a shared period of time. This gives me reason to ponder what our eternal relationship might have been. When I returned from a tour of the Holy Land, I realized that all of us in that particular group who traveled together and shared that common experience now have a bond of closeness that gives us a concern for each other. Whenever we see each other, it is as if we share a coming-home feeling because of that experience we shared in the Holy Land.

Putting that in an eternal perspective, it really makes me wonder and care deeply about you and each of my brothers and sisters. I consider you my fellow travelers. We are on our way back home together. Somehow that gives us a bond of closeness that ties us together. You and I are away from our heavenly home and our heavenly parents, traveling in a strange land. This life is a pilgrimage to a place far removed from our eternal home, but while we are away, we are blessed in having access to continuous communication and revelation.

On my desk is a little sign that reads "You are a child of

God. Call home." I really like that. On good days and not so good days, it's good to know that while we are away we can call home. I once heard a report that following an area conference, someone inquired of President Spencer W. Kimball, "With all you have on your mind, how do you ever get to sleep at night? Do you count sheep?" He reportedly replied, "No, I don't count sheep. I talk to the Shepherd." Wouldn't it be wonderful if each of us were not just to count sheep or list concerns, but rather talk to the Shepherd, to develop a close relationship so that in no circumstance do we ever feel we are traveling alone, for we are not.

Some years ago I learned a great lesson from another little journey. Actually it was just a little hike. My niece Shelly, then just six years old, started out on a hike with her parents. What was intended to be a three-mile hike turned out to be a fourteen-mile hike because her mother misread a sign. They were not seasoned travelers. As they came to the crest of a hill, when they realized that the trail was going to be much longer than they had anticipated, Shelly's mother determined to make the best of the situation and also make it a teaching opportunity. She explained to Shelly that this would be a good chance to see if they were made out of bricks or straw. The comparison had a familiar ring because of the favorite childhood story "The Three Little Pigs." She explained that their final destination was still their camp, so that while they had to go much farther than they had planned, at least they weren't lost and they knew where they were going. This sounded like an adventurous opportunity to Shelly. Though she didn't fully realize the drama of the situation, she was anxious to get on her way and find out, as she said, "what we're made of."

As with many teaching opportunities, the newness and novelty soon wore off. Then the real lessons and the real testing began. Driven by the desire to find out what she was really made of, this little six-year-old kept walking and walking. She welcomed the little periodic rests along the way, and as the day wore on, they became more frequent. Something within her nature would not let her give up. She just kept on walking. Near the end of the day, as the sun was setting and the water from the canteen was gone, and little Shelly's face was flushed and sunburned, she came up over a steep incline. Finally she stopped, ready to make an accounting to her parents. She paused a moment and then said, "Mom, I guess I'm made out of straw. I can't go any further." Her mother dropped down on her knee, wrapped her little girl in her arms, and said, "Honey, the camp is just around the corner. We've made it. You're made of brick."

Every so often that little girl, having grown a few years since then, will say, "Sure I can do it, because I'm made of brick."

Each of us has opportunities to find out what we're made of as we travel the sometimes steep inclines of life. I love the words of the song that says,

> *In the furnace God may prove thee,*
> *Thence to bring thee forth more bright,*
> *But can never cease to love thee,*
> *Thou art precious in his sight.*
> *God is with thee, God is with thee;*
> *Thou shalt triumph in his might.*
> —*Hymns, 1985, no. 43*

When we've gone as far as we can, we can be sure that the camp is in sight, and we won't be asked to go any further than we can. How far that is, how long the path or how hot the sun or how steep the climb may be, or when the end may come, I don't know. It is different for each of us. But of this I am sure: The path is too long, the trail too steep, the rocks too big, and the sun too hot for any one of us to make it back to camp alone. We will never reach home trying to walk by ourselves. That will come only as we develop faith in the Lord, Jesus Christ, and faith that He knows us and loves us individually, and when we walk with our hands in His, knowing that He will walk with us each step of the way if we will allow Him to. It is only when we choose to get off the path that we voluntarily separate ourselves from His companionship. But even then He offers His hand. He gave His life to ensure our safe return, but He won't force us to take hold, lest it thwart our progress.

Sometimes in our anxious uncertainties, our hearts might cry out and say, "Father, how much farther before it's enough? How many more steps must I take? Where is the camp? It's getting dark and late, and I feel far from home."

While standing on the banks of the river Jordan, I thought of Joshua leading all of Israel to that river and the great challenge they faced in crossing the water. As the great mass of people approached the river Jordan, the Lord spoke to Joshua and instructed him to go to the very brink and then to stand still. He was apparently telling Joshua what He is telling us—to go as far as we can and then stand still, stop, be calm, and listen to the voice from within. The Lord further told Joshua, "And it shall come to pass, as soon as the soles of the feet of the priests that bear the ark of the Lord, the Lord of all the earth, shall rest in the waters of Jordan, that the waters of Jordan shall be cut off from the waters that come down from above; and they shall stand upon an heap." We go to the brink, stand still, feel the Spirit, and then prepare to go just a little further if necessary. After Joshua had obeyed, we are told, "the priests that bare the ark of the covenant of the Lord stood firm on dry ground in the midst of Jordan, and all the Israelites passed over on dry ground." (See Joshua 3.)

The Lord tests us and tries us. He tests all of His saints. There is no question that the harder the test, the higher the reward for passing it. Abraham laid all that he had on the altar, thus proving himself worthy of exaltation. Our Father knows where we are on the path, and He knows when it is enough and when to provide the ram. We never walk alone. Because He loves us, He will not deprive us of the growth that comes from our tests, however hard they may be. It is comforting to know that He will never test any of us beyond our ability to withstand. We know that "there hath no temptation taken you but such as is common to man: but God is faithful, who will not suffer you to be tempted above that ye are able; but will with the temptation also make a way to escape, that ye may be able to bear it." (1 Corinthians 10:13.)

One of the really exciting things about reading the scriptures is to learn how our Father has cared about His children through the ages. We know that He will care about us no differently. We know what to expect, and our faith grows stronger because we know He is unchanging, and that His rules do not change. We know that He abides the law even when it must hurt Him dreadfully to see one of His children leave the path and wander off into dangerous territory.

Sometimes we may hear an anxious person crying out, "How could a loving father allow this to happen? It isn't fair." But it is because He is a loving father, and He gives us unwavering assurance that we can depend on Him, that it is fair. He does not change His mind or the rules. It is on this very principle that our faith must be built and will grow strong even if, in our shortsightedness, we might wish the rules could change just this once. We sing, "Lead kindly light, amid the encircling gloom. Lead thou me on. The night is dark and I am far from home." (*Hymns*, 1985, no. 97.) It is often in that very darkness, when there is no place else to turn, that we find our way to the Savior and come to know Him as we never would otherwise know Him.

In the book *Gospel Truth*, by President George Q. Cannon, I read one day what was an exciting truth for me. He said, "We humble people, we who feel ourselves sometimes so worthless, so good for nothing, we are not so worthless as we think. There is not one of us but what God's love has been expended upon. There is not one of us that He has not cared for and caressed. There is not one of us that He has not desired to save and that He has not devised means to save. There is not one of us that He has not given his angels charge concerning. We may be insignificant and contemptible in our eyes and in the eyes of others, but the truth remains that we are the children of God and that He has actually given His angels—invisible beings of power and might—charge concerning us and they watch over us and have us in their keeping." (*Gospel Truth,* pp. 1–2.)

Isn't that a wonderful thing to know? Maybe there are situations in our lives when we might be inclined to look heavenward and say of the guardian angels, "Where were you when I needed you?" But then there are other times when the Spirit whispers to us that surely our guardian angel must have been with us. Occasionally we might flippantly say, "Boy, your guardian angel must have been with you," when in fact we may be speaking a truth.

Sometimes when the sun is hot and the trail seems steep and it's the end of a long day, I have been known to go inside my home and close the door and say, "I don't want to have any more growing opportunities today." Isn't that always when the telephone rings or someone knocks at the door or maybe a child cries out in need of help, and we have another opportunity to keep going on? I believe that the progress that puts us closer in touch with our heavenly home is determined more by what happens on the inside than what takes place on the outside; what happens to the traveler rather than the conditions of the hurdles or even the detours along the path.

Our Father in heaven has surrounded us with evidences of His great love for us, even the air we breathe and the food we eat and the very path that we walk. Sometimes if we stumble and fall, we might find ourselves questioning whether or not He still loves us. Even while we are down, we have an opportunity to see things from a different perspective—beauties that are otherwise hidden.

A friend who likes to ski once told me that she has often observed that when skiers fall down, they usually become very frustrated. But occasionally she will notice someone who, after falling, lies quiet and calm, looking at the beauties all around. "When I made that observation," she said, "I almost anticipated my next fall because I wanted to lie there on my back and look up through the pine trees with the sun filtering down through them and see things I never had seen before. I have seen beautiful things I would not have seen had I not taken advantage of looking up when I was down."

Just as with Joshua, it is when we have gone as far as we can that we should stand still, remain calm, and listen to the quiet voice from within. As we observe evidences of our Father's hand in all creation and trust in the miracle that can come to pass in our lives after the trial of our faith, we can be calm enough for the Spirit to whisper to us.

Our Father's love for us is unconditional. It is not conditional upon our righteousness. He has told us, "If ye love me, keep my commandments," but His love for us is always unconditional, even when He must sometimes allow us to suffer the consequences of our wrong choices. It is when we come to know these things that we will have the courage to stand alone in defense of right, and when we will be able to help others find their way, even if the trail is steep and the sun hot and the camp temporarily out of sight.

On our way back home, there will be those along the way, just as with the good Samaritan on his way to Jericho, who will be in need of our help. As we become unwavering and unhalting in our direction and know who we are and, more important, whose we are, there will be others who will look to us to help guide them home safely. We will find ourselves traveling our own Jericho Road.

My sister Sharon tells it this way:

"A certain sister went down from her home to the supermarket and fell among thieves who stripped her of her confidence and self-esteem when she overheard them talking about her and her children, and they walked away, leaving her alone.

"And by chance there came down the aisle a certain lady dressed in fine clothes, and when she saw her, she passed down another grocery aisle.

"And likewise a lady who was a leader in the community, when she was at the place, came and looked on her and passed down another aisle without speaking.

"But a certain sister came down the aisle where she was, and when she saw her, she had compassion and went to her and bound up her wounds as she said, 'Let's go talk.'

"And at a time of doubt and discouragement, one sister ministered to another as she spoke of faith and hope and extended unconditional love—charity."

Occasionally when we may think we are guiding someone else along the path, we learn that in reality they were guiding us.

One spring day I was sitting in a fourth grade class, with the windows open, and all the world was coming into blossom outdoors. The children were sitting in their seats, busily doing their routine work. I pondered my responsibilities for these children and asked myself what curriculum was really important at that moment. Maybe because of the springtime or the scent of the blossoms in the air, suddenly the classroom routine was burdensome. I got up from my desk, walked to the chalkboard, and erased the arithmetic assignment on the board. Then I said softly to the children, "Please put your pencils down and clear your desks. Put everything away. We are going out of doors to experience life. I'd like you to take with you all of your senses. I'd like you to take with you your eyes and your ears and your mouth and your sense of touch."

I explained that we were going to go out to discover and explore and uncover and feel and hear and taste and sense all of life around us. I also asked that no one speak or interfere with anyone else's experience in nature. Then, when I gave them a signal, they were to come back in and write down their own feelings about their personal experience with life.

Outside I noticed one little boy sitting on the sidewalk and looking up at the sky. My impulse was to urge him to move around and to explore and experience, but I resisted. After an appropriate length of time I signaled to the children to come back in and invited them in a whisper to write on paper what they had experienced. In time the little boy who sat so still motioned to me. I went over to his desk, and he eagerly pushed his paper toward me and said, "Read mine." I read it in a whisper and it said, "I like blue. It's a place that never ends. It makes you feel like you could fall right through—blue." I realized that he had experienced the beauties of the sky that surrounds us in a way I had never realized. I was grateful that I had not interrupted his exploration into life to force him to experience what I was experiencing.

Another little child motioned to me. Her paper began, "Spring is a wonderful time of year. You can think. You can see. You can smell. You can hear." Her thoughts went on for a full page, unfolding her joy in nature.

I looked over at another little girl, Kristine. This was a child who always came to school late and said she liked the fourth grade because her teacher didn't yell at her when she came late; a little girl whose arms and elbows and lips were always chapped, whose dress was held together with a large safety pin, and whose hair was unkempt. I noticed that she was chewing on her pencil, struggling to find the words to express her feelings. Finally she gave a sign that said, "I want to share." I walked toward her desk and knelt down by her so that we would be on the same level, eye to eye. She was laboriously writing down the last word on a paper that had been erased so many times it was torn through. She handed it to me, and I read, "I never knowed the world looked so good." Kneeling beside her, which I thought was putting us at the same level, I realized she was much higher. I said in my heart and to her, "Thank you, Kristine. I never knowed the world looked so good either."

When we draw strength from within, we can see beauty everywhere. And we build that strength as we strive always to see God's hand in all that is good, in all of His creations. Every morning a new day is born, evidence of God's great love for us.

As we travel on our way back home and strive to follow the prophet, to study the scriptures, to pray for understanding, and to live the commandments, on occasion we will feel the overwhelming assurance of the close and sweet companionship of our Savior. And it will be so real that we will feel an ever-increasing desire to stay on the path until we reach home and rejoice again in that personal relationship that we once knew with Him.

On our way back home, may we come to know that with our Savior as our companion, we can make it. He made it possible. And we can expect to renew our friendships with those with whom we have shared the journey. "And the same sociality which exists among us here will exist among us there, only it will be coupled with eternal glory." (D&C 130:2.)

Chapter 18

Is It Okay to Believe Just One More Year?

A few years ago, my little niece approached her mother one December day as the spirit of Christmas began awakening. The gift-giving symbolized by Santa Claus and the other wonderful traditions were emerging with each new day. In a quiet moment away from the hustle and bustle, this little girl, with her heart full of childlike excitement and yet on the verge of growing up, cornered her mother and, in all soberness, posed this thoughtful question: "Mom, is it okay if I believe just one more year?"

In our grown-up world, sometimes we quit asking the questions because we are sure we already know the answers. And yet with each new year, there awakens within our hearts a yearning to reach far enough to somehow comprehend more fully the significance of that singular event, the birth of the Savior of the world and what it means to each one of us individually and collectively, as brothers and sisters, disciples, Latter-day Saints. Off in a quiet corner away from the hustle and bustle, we might well ask ourselves, What think I of Christ?

An unknown author makes this observation: "Though Christ a thousand times in Bethlehem be born / If He is not born in thee, thy soul is still forlorn." And even though we know the answer, consider with me this question: Is it okay if I believe just one more year?

In celebrating the event of the birth of our Savior, there are many pageants, plays, programs, and performances. Having taught elementary school for a number of years, I can personally give an account of a varied number of Josephs and Marys; and old bathrobes tucked up and tied around little bodies to give some resemblance of a shepherd; and angels with tinsel halos made from coat hangers mounted in such a way as to keep the haloes attached to the heads of the constantly moving little angels. You could always tell the wise men from the shepherds because they carried odd-shaped boxes adorned with jewels brought from home. Faithful parents would come: fathers in business suits looking as if they may have just slipped out from some large business meeting, and mothers and grandmothers sitting on little chairs far too small for comfort.

As a teacher, I would take my place midway between the performers and the audience. I never did quite determine where the greater performance was taking place. Was it on the makeshift stage or in the audience, where each pair of radiant eyes was riveted on performers as though each were doing a solo number?

Perhaps you are familiar with the school pageant where the little innkeeper forgot his lines and responded from his heart instead. When Joseph asked if there was room in the inn, the young innkeeper hesitated and the prompter whispered his lines from the wings: "There is no room. Be gone." The young innkeeper repeated the words. The young actor, Joseph, sadly placed his arm around Mary, and the two little people who had rehearsed their lines so well started to move away according to the script and the rehearsal. Suddenly this Christmas pageant became different from any other. "Don't go, Joseph," the innkeeper cried out. "Bring Mary back. She can have my room."

Contrary to the actual account of this event, for this pageant there was room in the inn. The room was in the innkeeper's own room; it was in his heart. The question we each must ask ourselves in our overcrowded lives: Is there room in the inn? Will we take the Savior into our life, into our heart, into our very soul, so that He becomes the center of our lives?

Late one evening the Christmas lights sparkled like jewels as we drove through the snow-packed streets to the outskirts of town. The lights were not as plentiful here, but each colorful bulb added beauty to the more humble homes nestled together in the gently falling snow. Driving down one street and then another, we tried with difficulty to read the street signs. Finally we found the address we were looking for. Making our way through the deep snow of the unshoveled walk, we rang the doorbell and were immediately greeted by Brent, an eight-year-old boy. He invited us in. The living room was small, but warm and cozy with a fire burning in the fireplace. The boy's eighty-six-year-old grandfather, with his leg in a cast, rested on the couch near the tree. He had slipped off the roof while attempting to shovel the heavy snow that had fallen the night before.

As we exchanged greetings and hugs, Brent stood anxiously waiting for the first opportunity to ask a question. In a most forthright and direct way he asked, "Have you ever shaken hands with the Prophet?" The eagerness with which he asked gave me reason to believe that he may have rehearsed that question in his mind several times in anticipation of our visit. "Yes, Brent," I said, "I have shaken the hand of the Prophet." "Oh," he said. His eyes were wide and his voice reminded me of what a great privilege that is. "If only I could just shake the hand of the Prophet," he went on. His tone suggested that should that be a possibility, it would surely be the greatest Christmas gift he could receive. And if not the greatest, at least it would be among the very best.

Sensing the love and respect Brent obviously felt for our Prophet, and wanting to somehow provide a tie between the Prophet and the young boy, I reached out my hand. "Brent," I said, "this hand has shaken the hand of the

Prophet." He grabbed my hand and shook it vigorously. Then he let go and turned his hand over from front to back to examine it thoroughly. "I'll never wash my hand," he said. Considering the problems this decision might cause, I suggested that he probably should wash his hand and just keep the memory in his mind. This suggestion was not acceptable. He had a better idea. "Okay," he said. "I'll wash my hand, but I'll save the water." That seemed like a good suggestion, although I supposed he was only joking.

Brent left the room. A few minutes later, he returned this time carrying a plastic bag dripping with water. Before anyone could question him, he proudly announced, "I washed my hand," holding up the bag full of water for all to see. We talked about the water in the bag and how that was a distant connection to the Prophet. Then our visit about Christmases past continued. Brent sat on the floor facing the Christmas tree, his knees peeking through his faded bluejeans, and from the corner of my eye I watched him examine the bag of water as if he were expecting to see some evidence that this was holy water. The fire burned low and the lights on the tree seemed to brighten.

After a few minutes, Brent got up and, taking his treasure with him, left the room. While I wondered if we would see him again before we left, he returned, this time without the plastic bag full of water. He had determined a better solution for his desire to be in touch with the Prophet. Standing in the doorway with his T-shirt wet all the way down the front, he explained what he had done. "I drank the water," he said.

This creative solution was not to be viewed as a joke or something to be made fun of. Brent was serious. He was carrying something important, not on the outside where he could lay it down, but on the inside. The water from the hand that he had washed, a hand that had shaken the hand of someone who had shaken the hand of the

Prophet, was now part of him, on the inside, and he would keep it. He made room on the inside.

Would it really make any difference? What did it really mean to Brent? It was much more than water, I was sure. But in the rush of the Christmas season, the incident slipped from my mind until a few days later. Then at sacrament meeting on the Sunday before Christmas, I received some understanding of what this young boy was feeling and wanting. The sacramental prayer had been offered and the sacred emblems were being passed quietly and reverently. The Sunday before Christmas brings a sensitivity that makes important things even more important, a time of recommitment and rededication, of sorrow for wrong doings, and of resolve and hope to do better in the new year. As the sister on my right passed the sacrament tray and held it while I raised the small cup of water to my lips, into my mind came this thought: "I want to get this water on the inside."

I thought of Brent, a newly baptized member. I remembered the baptismal covenant. I thought of the symbolism of the water, the washing away of our sins. The cup of water of which I would partake renewed the promises and blessings of the atonement of Jesus Christ. It was His birth we were celebrating. I could hear in my mind again the sacramental prayer on the water: " . . . that they do always remember him, that they may have his Spirit to be with them. Amen." The water symbolizes His blood, which was shed for each of us so that we might live and have eternal life. "Thank you, Brent," I said to myself, "for this wonderful gift you have given me: an increased desire to drink the water, the symbolism of His atonement, to get it on the inside, to make room in my life for Him so that I might become more like Him."

To the question from Brent, "Have you ever shaken hands with the Prophet?" my answer is yes. But I have also shaken hands with a little eight-year-old boy, and I've learned important and eternal truths from both.

President Marion G. Romney gave us great insight when he explained, "Now there is a doctrine abroad in the world today which teaches that the physical emblems of the sacrament are transformed into the flesh and blood of Jesus. We do not teach such doctrine, for we know that any transformation which comes from the administration of the sacrament takes place in the souls of those who understandingly partake of it. It is the participating individuals who are affected, and they are affected in a most marvelous way, for they are given the Spirit of the Lord to be with them." (*Conference Report*, April 1946, p. 40.)

In the spring of 1980, my husband and I went up from Galilee, out of the city of Nazareth, into Judea, unto the town of Bethlehem. We walked the paths where Jesus walked and felt His presence there. We stood beneath the gnarled olive trees in the Garden of Gethsemane, where the Savior of the world suffered and shed drops of blood.

As we looked on the brow of the hill at Golgotha, we could hear in our minds the words, "Father, forgive them, for they know not what they do." We envisioned the setting of the Last Supper, where He may have been thinking of the imminent events that were to follow, and where He taught His apostles and gave the commandment to love one another. We thought of Him moving up the streets of the old city and carrying the cross toward Golgotha, because there was no room for Him in the hearts of the persecutors. In the quiet of that hour, we each asked ourselves, "Why did He do this all for me? How in God's name can I ever pay?" And we wondered if we, like the innkeeper, would call, "Come back, come back. You can have my room. My heart. My time. My life. My vote. I give it all. All that I have. All that I am. All that I ever hope to be."

Oh yes, it is okay to believe one more year and another and another and another. We believe in God, the Eternal Father, and in His Son, Jesus Christ, and in the Holy Ghost. We believe that through the atonement of Christ, all mankind may be saved through obedience to the laws and ordinances of the gospel. At those very times when we feel least worthy, least comfortable about carrying His holy name and have a keener sense of our imperfections—those moments when the flesh is weak and our spirits suffer disappointments knowing what we can become—we might feel a sense of withdrawing, a pulling away, a feeling of needing to set aside for a time at least that divine relationship with the Savior until we are more worthy. It is at that very moment, even in our unworthiness, that the offer is again given to us to accept the great gift of the atonement, even before we change. When we feel the need to pull away, we can reach out to Him. Instead of feeling the need to resist, we can submit to His will and partake of His gifts. What do we give in return? Love to one another. Then as our faith grows stronger, His Spirit fills our hearts. The Light of Christ burns brightly, and we take upon us His countenance.

Chapter 19

Fruits of Faith

According to Dr. Hugh Nibley, an ancient writer once asked: " 'Who is man . . . that he should take his place before thy face? . . . How can the clay and the potter sit together; or who understands the wonderful plan of God?' And he supplies the answer: 'For eternal glory he has chosen me, and for that he teaches me. . . . 'The Way of Light itself is 'the spirit of the understanding of all the Plan. . . . Without thee nothing came into existence—and he instructed me in all knowledge.' " (*Nibley on the Timely and the Timeless* [Salt Lake City: Publishers Press, 1978], p. 33.)

It is through the gospel of Jesus Christ, the plan of salvation, that the way is provided for each of us to one day sit down with the potter, the Creator, even God our Father and His Son, Jesus Christ, and to be one with them and like them, the ultimate fruit of faith.

In the winter of 1834–35, seven lectures on faith were presented to a class of the elders of the Church in Kirtland, Ohio. The seventh of these lectures presents important principles that relate to the fruits of faith. To help us better understand faith and how it works in our lives, let us examine three of these principles: (1) faith brings an eternal perspective to our mortal life; (2) salvation is the result of faith; and (3) perfection comes through faith.

1. *Faith brings an eternal perspective to our mortal life.*

In the seventh lecture we read:

"The whole visible creation, as it now exists, is the effect of faith. It was by which faith it was framed, and it is by the power of faith that it continues in its organized form. . . . So, then, faith is truly the first principle in the science of THEOLOGY, and, when understood, leads the mind back to the beginning, and carries it forward to the end; or, in other words, from eternity to eternity. . . . All the blessings of eternity are the effects of faith.

"From this we may extend as far as any circumstances may require, whether on earth or in heaven, and we will find it the testimony of all inspired men, or heavenly messengers, that all things that pertain to life and godliness are the effects of faith and nothing else; all learning, wisdom and prudence fail, and every thing else as a means of salvation but faith." (*Lectures on Faith* [Deseret Book, 1985], 7:5–6, 20.)

Faith is literally the power by which God Himself operates in earthly and heavenly affairs. Miracles are the fruits of faith; faith precedes the miracle. Behind each miracle is divine power, and that power is faith.

As a young girl I overheard the doctors explain to my parents, after I had had a serious mastoid operation, that I would not only lose my hearing but also my equilibrium and thus the ability to walk. My name was placed on the prayer roll in the temple, and my father, assisted by another Melchizedek Priesthood bearer, gave me a blessing—and with faith in God, I knew I would be healed.

Faith is a principle, a key of power, that opens the door to our progress. The abundance of life and salvation can come to us only through our faith. It is the source of our feeling of well-being, of courage, and of peace both in this life and in the world to come. If we begin with Adam and look through all the history of the generations of this earth, we see his descendants (ourselves included) receiving blessings and privileges according to the degree of faith that they possess.

The restoration of the gospel of Jesus Christ began with the faith of one young boy. He had studied the scriptures. He had implicit trust in the words of God: "If any of you lack wisdom, let him ask of God, that giveth to all men liberally, and upbraideth not; and it shall be given him. But let him ask in faith, nothing wavering." (James 1:5–6.) Of that scripture he recorded, "Never did any passage of scripture come with more power to the heart of man than this did at this time to mine." (Joseph Smith—History 1:2.) One beautiful spring morning in a grove of trees near his home, Joseph Smith knelt in prayer. He prayed vocally for the first time and asked God a specific question. His prayer of faith unlocked the heavens. By the power of faith, the Father and His Son appeared to Joseph Smith, called him by name, and instructed him. That same invitation to ask God in faith is extended to each of us today; and because of the restoration of the gospel of Jesus Christ, we know of the nature of God, the love of God, the reality of God, and the great plan of salvation provided for us, His children, to return and once again dwell with Him.

Some time ago, I was asked to speak to a group of young women on an early morning in the high Uintah mountains of eastern Utah. At the conclusion of my remarks, I reminded them that the Prophet Joseph Smith went into a grove of trees and prayed in faith. I suggested, "Each one of you, sometime before returning home, find a quiet spot in nature where you can experience reverence for life all around you, and talk with your Father in heaven. Share with Him the things that are in your heart. He is always available, and He will hear you."

Two weeks later in a fast and testimony meeting in her own ward, Becky, the assistant youth camp director, stood to bear her testimony. "Something about the feelings I had that special morning made me want to be alone for a while," she said. "So I found a private spot where there was a little opening in the trees. When I knelt down on the ground, thick with pine needles, I didn't know for sure what to say, so I closed my eyes and said, 'Heavenly Father, do you know I am here?' I waited and waited, and I could hear the wind in the trees. Then I opened my eyes and saw the sun coming through the leaves, and I felt all warm inside." She paused a moment and then, in a reverent whisper, added, "You may not think it was anything, but I know he knew I was there."

Becky, like the Prophet Joseph Smith, had faith in God. She felt that her request was appropriate. She simply asked, "Do you know I'm here?" and she received an immediate answer. As she left the mountains she was never the same again. She knew more about God than she had ever known before. She could better understand the testimony of the Prophet, that God did hear and answer his prayer.

Do we know He knows we are here? Have we asked? Through communication with God and by the power of faith, Becky learned for herself that God is real. He cares about us, His children. He hears our prayers. He answers to our spirits with a message that speaks louder than words. While others may not be impressed or believe, by the power of faith we can *know* that He knows we are here. And with that assurance, we have the first requirement necessary to develop that faith which leads to salvation: we know for ourselves that God lives.

We live in a time when people's hearts are failing them and they need greater faith and a deeper understanding of God's eternal purposes. The burdens of life can be lifted through faith, but without it people are unsettled, unsure, and unsaved. Skepticism, cynicism, and doubt run rampant as the world ripens in iniquity, and they would, if possible, destroy faith and its fruits. In the absence of faith, the darkest clouds of fear and depression close in and put out the light.

Young Latter-day Saints are showing evidence of the quality of faith that will carry them through difficult times and prepare them to meet their God. A young woman in

Anchorage, Alaska, one of many thousands of young women of the Church who wrote messages, tied them to balloons, and sent them soaring into the sky, shares the testimony she wrote: "I am 15 years old and a member of The Church of Jesus Christ of Latter-day Saints. I know that God lives and loves us. Jesus Christ is the Savior of the world. I love them with all my heart. If I could wish for anything for the world, I would wish that everyone had a sure knowledge that God lives and that he hears and answers prayers. I'm thankful for the answers I've received to my prayers. You too can receive answers to your prayers. All you have to do is ask. No matter who you are or what you have done, God will listen."

With faith in God and a knowledge that He listens to the prayers of His children, this young woman, with hundreds of others, is bearing strong testimony. Their faith will keep them on course as they walk the straight and narrow path leading to salvation.

2. *Salvation is the result of faith.*

"Who cannot see, then, that salvation is the effect of faith? for . . . all the heavenly beings work by this principle; and it is because they are able so to do that they are saved, for nothing but this could save them. And this is the lesson which the God of heaven, by the mouth of his holy prophets, has been endeavouring to teach to the world. Hence we are told that 'Without faith it is impossible to please God'; and that salvation is of faith, that it might be by grace; to the end the promise might be sure to all the seed. (Romans 4:16.)" (*Lectures on Faith* 7:17.)

What is the relationship between faith and salvation? The answer is found in what the Savior proposed to the human family when he provided a means to save them: "He proposed to make them like unto himself, and he was like the Father, the great prototype of all saved beings; and for any portion of the human family to be assimilated into their likeness is to be saved; and to be unlike them is to be destroyed; and on this hinge turns the door of salvation." (*Lectures on Faith* 7:16.)

Our diligent effort to plant the seed of faith and nourish it daily is the most significant thing we can pursue in this life. It gives us life. It is the very breath of life. It is the purpose of life. Elder Bruce R. McConkie stated, "We are on a course that calls for us to pursue faith, and we have to pursue it until that faith is perfected in us, meaning until we have the degree and quality and kind of power that God our Father possesses." (Address to Brigham Young University student body, October 31, 1967.)

The plan of salvation revealed in these latter days includes all that is needed for us to return to our Father in heaven and live with Him once again, but it unfolds gradually to each of us according to our diligence and faith in following the plan. Faith and salvation are linked together. As mortals we are in the process of ultimately gaining salvation. Faith possesses qualities that move us forward toward that ultimate goal.

According to one writer, "*Faith is active.* [It] will impel to action. . . . *Faith is specific.* . . . [It] is vested in, and has force and power as it relates to particular individuals, teachings, principles, and relationships. *Faith is individual.* . . . As a principle of growth and action it must be won, with the help and power of God, by each within himself. . . . *Faith is spiritual insight.* [It is] 'the evidence of things not seen' (Hebrews 11:1). . . . *Faith is assurance.* It is a feeling of inner certainty. . . . From such a feeling of assurance the ancient psalmist exclaimed, 'The Lord is my light and my salvation; whom shall I fear? The Lord is my strength of my life; of whom shall I be afraid?' (Psalm 27:1). *Faith is creative.* [It] moves men to solve problems, to find solutions, to ask questions believing that there are answers to be found. . . . *Faith is divine companionship.* He who has faith in a Divine Father is never alone. Faith in God carries with it the promise of divine companionship." (Wendall O. Rich, *Our Living Gospel* [Bookcraft, 1964], pp. 70–73.)

It is the remarkable reality of the promise of this divine companionship that fills our souls in peaceful and troubled times and assures us we are never alone. We have covenanted with God and He with us. When we went into the waters of baptism and covenanted to keep His commandments, He also covenanted with us that He would never desert us, never leave us, but that we could always have His Spirit to be with us. It is faith in this companionship with the Lord Jesus Christ and obedience to His commandments that allows us to endure all of the vicissitudes of this mortal sojourn so necessary for our spiritual growth.

We see the great power of faith in the lives of our brothers and sisters in various degrees and in various circumstances. This unseen but very real force often appears more evident during times of trial and testing. President Pablo Choc of the Patzicia Branch in Guatemala was one whose faith was tried. While attending a funeral for a fifteen-year-old Mormon boy, he was impressed by the Spirit, and afterwards he asked the missionaries to stay and teach him. He was subsequently baptized, and in time he was called to serve as branch president. His story was reported in the *Church News:*

"But his service to his fellowman was never greater than during the 1976 Guatemalan earthquake. At the same time the fearsome earthquake was knocking the supporting beam on top of Elder Randall Ellsworth while the young missionary was sleeping in the Patzicia Branch cultural hall, it was tumbling the walls of Pres. Choc's home, killing his wife, a young son and daughter. After he had seen to the needs of his family, and taken care of the bodies of his wife and two children, Pres. Choc immediately went to the branch chapel to check on the damage there. At the building he assisted in freeing Elder Ellsworth and helped transport the missionary to Guatemala City for medical aid, knowing all the while that his beloved wife and children lay dead back in Patzicia."

Later, President Choc shared his feelings. "I am of

course saddened by the death of my wife and children," he said, "and I will miss her in helping to raise our six remaining children. We were married very young, and in all those years of marriage we never had a real problem. Then in the three weeks after her death I did a lot of praying to the Lord, more than I had ever done before, and I found a lot of strength in my prayers and felt myself getting closer to the Lord. . . . Because of this, I don't think my faith ever weakened or wavered for a moment."

Elder Choc's eldest son, Daniel, was serving on a mission at the time, teaching the Mayan dialect to missionaries from America so proselyting could be stepped up in the mission district. These missionaries were assigned to assist the Saints in their area in cleaning up after the earthquake. While Elder Choc was cleaning up the inside of a home, an aftershock occurred. His companion and two other missionaries scrambled to safety, but Elder Choc was trapped by a falling wall and killed. "I was sad, very sad when Daniel was killed," President Choc recalled, "but in a way I am very happy. There are so many of my Mayan people on the other side that Daniel, his mother and the other two children are spending their time teaching them the Gospel message in their native language, and they are spending their time serving the Lord. This is really the Lord's work." (*Church News,* April 23, 1977, p. 5.)

It is with faith in God that we are able to face the events of this life. We do this on a daily basis as we attend to the routine happenings, hardly recognizing the vital moving force that accompanies our comings and goings. However, like the ebb and flow of the waters on the shoreline, there come occasions of high tide when the power of faith is activated in ways that we recognize as miracles, and they become the very fruits of faith. They bear evidence of the realities of God and our relationship to Him. It is then, from a reservoir of faith gradually accumulated over years of learning and living the gospel and coming to know the Savior, that we can draw deeply. With unwavering faith in

God and the righteous desire of our hearts, we can call upon the Lord and actually witness His hand in our own personal lives. I know this to be true.

President Harold B. Lee, speaking to seminary leaders at a meeting at Brigham Young University, declared, "Yes, the Savior, too, is in our midst. His eyes are upon us, but we can't always see him. But the day can come when we could see him. It isn't the Lord who withholds himself from us; it is we who withhold ourselves from him. And if we were living completely worthy, we could see him and have a personal visitation and we would have the assurance, even though we couldn't see him, that he was there, walking, talking, listening, aiding, directing. Make no mistake—this is his work." (L. Brent Goates, *Harold B. Lee, Prophet and Seer* [Bookcraft, 1985], pp. 319–20.)

We would expect to see such faith among the prophets. But we may also see it in the lives of all of His children who truly believe.

Recently I received a letter from the thirteen-year-old president of a Beehive class. This young girl, called of God and set apart by the authority of His holy priesthood, wrote: "This past month has been a real trial for me. Dealing with my grandfather's death, then my mother is in the hospital, and then my grandma died. All within a month's time.

"I now realize the power and influence that I have with the Beehive girls, and the difference I can make in their lives. I love this gospel, and I will strive to live the commandments of God all my life. I know that I'm a daughter of a Heavenly Father who loves me, and I love him. I will stand as a witness of God at all times, in all things, and in all places. . . . I will be prepared to make and keep sacred covenants, receive the ordinances of the temple, and enjoy the blessings of exaltation! I hope that I can always be an example to others that they might be touched by my strong testimony of the gospel.

"I hope that I can find the lost sheep of the Lord's flock.

I *will* stand for truth and righteousness. I *will* hold my torch high for everyone to see that I love the Lord and his gospel."

It is a great comfort to know that we can walk each day by faith. The prophet Alma speaks words of hope and encouragement: "Behold, if ye will awake and arouse your faculties, even to an experiment upon my words, and exercise a particle of faith, yea, even if ye can no more than desire to believe, let this desire work in you, even until ye believe in a manner that ye can give place for a portion of my words."

Then comes the glory and absolute promise:

"And because of your diligence and your faith and your patience with the word in nourishing it, that it may take root in you, behold, by and by ye shall pluck the fruit thereof, which is most precious, which is sweet above all that is sweet, and which is white above all that is white, yea, and pure above all that is pure; and ye shall feast upon this fruit even until ye are filled, that ye hunger not, neither shall ye thirst.

"Then, my brethren, ye shall reap the rewards of your faith, and your diligence, and patience, and long-suffering, waiting for the tree to bring forth fruit unto you." (Alma 32:27, 42–43.)

The example of Enos provides a guide for each of us as we seek diligently. First, he remembered what he had been taught; then he went before God with a specific desire. The words of his father regarding eternal life sank into his heart. His soul hungered. He cried out in mighty prayer. He was answered by the voice of the Lord and received a remission of his sins. He asked how it was done and was taught that it came because of faith in Christ. His faith in the Lord became unshaken. He continued to pray, now in behalf of his brethren. The Lord said, "I will grant unto thee according to thy desires, because of thy faith. . . . Whatsoever thing ye shall ask in faith, believing that ye shall receive in the name of Christ, ye shall receive it." (Enos 1:12, 15.)

These steps were then followed with this promise to Enos: "I soon go to the place of my rest, which is with my Redeemer; for I know that in him I shall rest. And I rejoice in the day when my mortal shall put on immortality, and shall stand before him; then shall I see his face with pleasure, and he will say unto me: Come unto me, ye blessed, there is a place prepared for you in the mansions of my Father." (Enos 1:27.)

After praying and pondering, we become attuned to promptings that help us discern truth from error and that bring thoughts to our minds. Promptings come as surely as we live from day to day. To this I testify. We can hear the words and thoughts as they are formulated in our minds. We can learn to recognize promptings when they come. They are usually fleeting and faint, never imposed.

I have always known the power of faith and prayer. But since my call as Young Women general president, I know it more surely than I have known before, perhaps because I have sought more diligently, more earnestly, more fervently. My prayers have been more specific. There are occasions after I have inquired of the Lord concerning important matters that words and thoughts have filled my mind. I have taken a pencil and pad and attempted to record all the insights and impressions as quickly as I can. Many times those very thoughts and words have been significant to my assignment. As we, our Father's children, have these undeniable experiences, is it any wonder we find ourselves striving, yearning, reaching to feel the operation of the Spirit of the Lord upon our spirits regularly and, if possible, constantly?

As we strive to increase our faith in God and gain knowledge through our own experiences, often the hardest thing to do is to believe in our own worthiness, our personal righteousness. Is there a soul alive who has not had an occasion to cry out and plead with God at some time, with a burning desire to increase in personal righteousness, to reach and stretch far enough to connect? We not only yearn to know how to call upon the Lord in faith, but also desire to do everything possible to activate the power of faith. Often, after extended periods of fasting and prayer, have we not asked, "But, Father, what more can I do? What should I understand about working by faith?" At those very times when we may feel least worthy and least comfortable in calling upon the Lord in faith, when we have a keener sense of our imperfections, when the flesh is weak and our spirit suffers disappointments knowing the frailties of our lives are shouting at us, in those moments our faith may waver. It is then, after we have expended our own best efforts, that we must trust in the Lord completely to compensate for our weaknesses.

Our Savior, in His great understanding and love for each of us, has promised, "I will not leave you comfortless." (John 14:18.) Through the process of cleansing our souls, when we have become meek and lowly of heart, then "cometh the visitation of the Holy Ghost, which Comforter filleth with hope and perfect love." (Moroni 8:26.) Christ "inviteth all to come unto him and partake of his goodness; and he denieth none that come unto him." (2 Nephi 26:33.) With this hope, and being in tune with the Holy Spirit, we can be guided each day of our lives. As our ability increases, our capacity and desire increase, and we grow "grace for grace." (See D&C 93:20.)

As we face each day and seriously consider those things that are worthy of our attention, we learn to exercise our faith every day. Matters of concern calling for increased faith might include such things as a desire to strengthen our faith, strengthen family relationships, increase understanding and sensitivity to the gift of the Holy Ghost, increase physical health, study scriptures, magnify Church callings, continue in education, or increase employment skills. Through prayer and the promptings of the Spirit, we can develop our own personalized list according to our individual needs.

Elder Bruce R. McConkie counseled, "Don't go out and try to move mountains, but go out and start in a small degree to do the thing you need to do in your life to get what you ought to have temporally and spiritually. . . . Work on the projects ahead, and when you have taken one step in the acquiring of faith, it will give you the assurance in your soul that you can go forward and take the next step, and by degrees your power or influence will increase until eventually, in this world or in the next, you will say to the Mt. Zerins in your life, 'Be thou removed.' You will say to whatever encumbers your course of eternal progress, 'Depart,' and it will be so." (Address at Brigham Young University, October 31, 1967.)

3. *Perfection Comes Through Faith.*

Let us consider those things that may not move a mountain right away but will move us forward toward a more complete faith. Again we must ask, "What should I understand about working by faith?" The answer: "We understand that when a man works by faith he works by mental exertion instead of physical force. It is by words, instead of exerting his physical powers, with which every being works when he works by faith." (*Lectures on Faith* 7:3.)

Prayer takes mental exertion. We need to learn to access power by pleading our cause in words that are specific to our needs. We also need to take time to ponder and meditate. Our Father in heaven has promised that when we diligently seek and then ask and knock, the door to heaven shall be opened unto us. (See D&C 88:63.) We first have the desire, then seek and draw upon our personal experiences. We search for additional enlightenment and edification in an effort to expand our understanding. We study the principles of the gospel and consider how they might be related to the question at hand.

Thought allows us to create, to envision, to experience

something in our mind. When we see clearly and become specific about what we are seeking and feel that it is a righteous desire and according to the will of God, we can focus our thinking with a concentration of power so that our faith, the energy of our mental processes, can be brought to bear upon the thing for which we are praying. Through prayer we can then call upon the power of heaven, the enabling power that allows us to exercise our faith. That is why we are counseled to keep our eye single to His glory; in doing so, our "minds become single to God." (See D&C 88:67–68.)

As a young girl, I worried about the importance of gaining knowledge. In anguish I asked my father, "If the glory of God is intelligence and you are not smart, what will happen to you?" And my very wise and learned father, who never graduated from high school but was self-taught and intelligent through diligent study and great faith, eased my concern when he explained, "My dear child, if you are diligent in your studies and do your very best and are obedient to God's commandments, one day, when you enter the holy temple, the university of the Lord, you will be prepared in your mind and spirit to learn and know all you need to know to return to your Father in heaven." Faith in that promise seemed to unlock my mind. Study and faith were then put to work together, and over time, after plodding toil, whole-souled devotion, and mental exertion, the realization of the Lord's promise came.

And after the trial of our faith, what can we expect? Salvation, the greatest gift of all the gifts of God, the most glorious of all the fruits of faith. "When men begin to live by faith they begin to draw near to God; and when faith is perfected they are like him; and because he is saved they are saved also; for they will be in the same situation he is in, because they have come to him; and when he appears they shall be like him, for they will see him as he is." (*Lectures on Faith* 7:8.)

Elder McConkie taught that "to be saved is to be like

Christ, inheriting, receiving, and possessing as he does. To gain salvation is to grow in faith until we have the faith of Christ and thus are like him. Our nearness to him and to salvation is measured by the degree of our faith. To gain faith is to attain the power of Christ, which is God's power. To believe in Christ in the full and true sense is to 'have the mind of Christ' (1 Corinthians 2:16), that is, to believe what he believes, think what he thinks, say what he says, and do what he does. It is to be one with him by the power of the Holy Ghost." (*A New Witness for the Articles of Faith* [Deseret Book, 1985], pp. 206–7.)

Lest we become discouraged, it is important to understand and remember the process by which we grow spiritually. It is not intended that we reach perfection in this life. On one occasion Joseph Smith made the following declaration, "When you climb up a ladder, you must begin at the bottom, and ascend step by step, until you arrive at the top; and so it is with the principles of the Gospel—you must begin with the first, and go on until you learn all the principles of exaltation. But it will be a great while after you have passed through the veil before you will have learned them. It is not all to be comprehended in this world; it will be a great work to learn our salvation and exaltation even beyond the grave." (*Teachings of the Prophet Joseph Smith,* p. 348.)

Many scriptures refer to the Savior's statement that He came to fulfill His Father's will. Our purpose is to make our will the same as His will. As we feast upon the words of Christ through earnest study and come to know His will, then humble ourselves and learn to bend our will as well as our knees, our faith increases, becoming stronger. We have an ever-increasing desire to want to carry out His will, and we become able and anxious to follow the pattern set by the Nephites: "They did fast and pray oft, and did wax stronger and stronger in their humility, and firmer and firmer in the faith of Christ, unto the filling their souls with joy and consolation, yea, even to the purifying and the sanctification of their hearts, which sanctification cometh because of their yielding their hearts unto God." (Helaman 3:35.)

To the reality of this principle and power of faith leading us to salvation, I bear my personal witness. I watched a man of great faith experience the precious fruits of quiet submission, peace, and spiritual confidence as he faced the final stages of his mortal probation. Not many years ago, my father, who then lived with us, was diagnosed as having cancer. Following his surgery, he came home from the hospital, weak in body but undaunted in spirit.

Over the next many weeks I saw his body steadily weaken. It was as though his spirit was magnified by his increased faith as his body steadily wasted away. Sometimes I would wait outside his bedroom door while he was on his knees for what often seemed a very long time and pondered the two-way communication I knew was taking place. His meals consisted of a spoonful of baby food— all he could manage. But he expressed thanks for it and gratitude for the lessons of each day.

He taught us continually as he prepared himself for what he referred to as his graduation. At his last fast and testimony meeting, he spoke only briefly, quoting Mosiah concerning the need to yield to the enticings of the Holy Spirit and to become "as a child, submissive, meek, humble, patient, full of love, willing to submit to all things which the Lord seeth fit to inflict upon him, even as a child doth submit to his father." (Mosiah 3:19.)

A few days later Dad stayed in bed, sleeping off and on during the day. I decided to sit with him. It seemed his eyes were open, yet he wasn't seeing me. I took his hand in mine, a hand that had spanked me and blessed me and caressed me throughout my life. "Dad," I whispered. He didn't respond. "If you know I'm here, please squeeze my hand." I wasn't sure if there was a squeeze, but it didn't seem like it. I bent over and put my cheek next to his very bony cheek, with my hand on the other side of his face. I waited just a second, then straightened up. It was as though his gaze returned from a long way off. He looked at me just a moment, and in his eyes I saw complete peace. Joy, trust, confidence, and anticipation all mingled together in that look. A tear escaped from the corner of his eye. I pressed my cheek to his again. There are things we cannot find words or even sounds to express, but in that moment we spoke spirit to spirit, and I knew he knew God was near.

Shortly after, my father's eternal spirit left his mortal body. We as a family gathered together. I had seen what had taken place, but what I felt was more real than what I saw. Dad was not there in the body, but he was there with us, extending his great strength that had sustained us over the years. We knelt by his bed to give thanks. With tears of gratitude binding us together as a family, we knew that, because of what we had experienced but could not explain, we understood and felt that peace of which he had so often spoken—that peace which passeth all understanding.

Yes, the plan of salvation gives meaning and direction, vision and hope. It is with faith in God that we begin and end this mortal life. God is our Father. We are His children, and to become like Him is our eternal quest, our destiny. While this striving for perfection will continue on after this life, we can witness evidence of the great saving power of faith and its fruits all along the journey. Of these eternal truths, I bear my personal witness.

Index

About the Author

Ardeth Greene Kapp, who was born and reared in Glenwood, Alberta, Canada, received a bachelor's degree in education from the University of Utah and a master's degree in curriculum development from Brigham Young University. She has been an elementary school teacher and a college instructor and the writer and instructor for a television series.

Much of Sister Kapp's church service has been with youth programs, including the Primary, Sunday School, and young women's organizations. For several years she was a member of the Youth Correlation Committee, and from 1971 to 1978 she was a member of the general presidency of the Young Women. She was sustained as general president of that organization on April 7, 1984. She and her husband, Heber B. Kapp, reside in Bountiful, Utah.

Other books by Sister Kapp include *Miracles in Pinafores and Bluejeans, The Gentle Touch, All Kinds of Mothers, Echoes from My Prairie,* and *I Walk by Faith.*